"Dan Becker's book is a great blen[...] and principled politics; it is certain to cause us to rethink prolife strategy in the 21st century."

Dr. Donald Wildmon
Founder and Chairman Emeritus of
American Family Association and American Family Radio

"The push for personhood across the United States is motivating the prolife movement while also inspiring others to take up the cause. Dan Becker has been out front in leading the personhood charge and his book gives special insight on how we can all work together to make the US a true prolife nation."

Tom McClusky
Senior Vice President
Family Research Council Action

"All believers in God should insist, without compromise, that the human law must always treat every innocent human being as a person entitled to the right to life. Dan Becker courageously affirms this truth."

Professor Charles Rice
Emeritus Professor of Law
University of Notre Dame

"Dan Becker's book provides a much needed challenge to those in the prolife movement who are content with the status quo; it is a strong reminder that we should never compromise principle when defending what Pope John Paul II described as "the inviolable right of every innocent human being to life."

Robert J. Muise
Senior Trial Counsel
Thomas More Law Center

"I just got around to reading your book tonight, and I think I won't stop until I am done. It is the finest prolife work I have read, period."

Gualberto Jones
Executive Director
Personhood Colorado

"The field of bio-science brings a host of unforeseen public policy issues that adversely impact our "unalienable right to life." Legal Personhood is at the root of all dialogue and debate. The prolife movement can no longer focus solely on abortion, but must expand to include the new challenges brought on by the emerging technology of the twenty-first century.

I commend the Personhood movement and its political successes as a consistent and promising approach to restoring respect and effective legal protection to all innocent human life from its earliest biological beginning until natural death."

Morton Blackwell
Founder
Leadership Training Institute

"Brilliant! Personhood is the core of the prolife battle in the 21st century, I have not seen this articulated better than by Dan Becker in this book. Fighting for the Personhood rights of the preborn is common sense, it works and it is righteous. This book is a must read for anyone serious about ending abortion and restoring dignity to the human race."

Keith Mason
Co-Founder
Personhood USA

Personhood

A PRAGMATIC GUIDE TO PROLIFE
VICTORY IN THE 21ST CENTURY
AND THE RETURN TO FIRST
PRINCIPLES IN POLITICS

DANIEL C. BECKER

TKS Publications
Alpharetta, Georgia

TKS Publications
777 Rivendell Lane, Alpharetta, GA 30004
World Wide Web: www.tkspublications.com
Email: email@tkspublications.com

Copyright © 2011 by Daniel C. Becker
All rights reserved.

Unless otherwise indicated, all Scripture quotations are from The Holy Bible, English Standard Version® (ESV®), copyright © 2001 by Crossway, a publishing ministry of Good News Publishers. Used by permission. All rights reserved.

Chapter 9 is a work of fiction. All characters appearing in this work are fictitious. Any resemblance to real persons, living or dead, is purely coincidental.

Cover Photo: *Twins,* Getty Images Collection: Brand X Pictures, Photographer: Steve Allen

---

ISBN-13: 978-0-983190-30-1

Printed in the United States of America

Library of Congress Control Number: 2010942357

REL012110	RELIGION / Christian Life / Social Issues
REL084000	RELIGION / Religion, Politics & State
POL043000	POLITICAL SCIENCE / Political Process / Political Advocacy
SOC046000	SOCIAL SCIENCE / Abortion & Birth Control

In the United Kingdom

HRAM2	Religion and politics
HRAM1	Religious ethics
JFMA	Ethical issues: abortion and birth control

Revision

28 27 26 25 24 23 22 21 20 19 18 17 16 15 14 13 12 11 10 9 8 7 6 5 4 3 2 1

To all my co-laborers at Georgia Right to Life who have labored selflessly and faithfully for those who cannot speak for themselves, you are indeed a voice for the voiceless,

And to my best friend, in life and in love;
"Sweetheart, I haven't given up the fight."

In Memoriam

Susan Dianne Becker
July 4, 1954–February 28, 2006

Policy, however, Sir, is not my principle, and I am not ashamed to say it. There is a principle above everything that is politic, and when I reflect on the command which says: "Thou shalt do no murder," believing its authority to be divine, how can I dare to set up any reasonings of my own against it?

William Wilberforce

For since, in the wisdom of God, the world did not know God through wisdom, it pleased God through the folly of what we preach to save those who believe. For Jews demand signs and Greeks seek wisdom, but we preach Christ crucified, a stumbling block to Jews and folly to Gentiles, but to those who are called, both Jews and Greeks, Christ the power of God and the wisdom of God.

1 Corinthians 1:21–24

Contents

Preface *11*

Chapter 1 Personhood, Prudence, and Pragmatism without
                Compromise *21*

Chapter 2 Personhood: A Roadmap to Victory *31*

Chapter 3 Personhood: A Biblical Necessity *47*

Chapter 4 Personhood: Principled Pragmatism *65*

Chapter 5 Personhood: Future of the Prolife Movement *73*

Chapter 6 Personhood: Prudential, Political and Legal Objections *81*

Chapter 7 Personhood: How Can I Start the Process in My State? *101*

Chapter 8 Personhood: The Battle is the Lord's *117*

Chapter 9 Personhood: What Is at Stake If We Fail? *129*

Appendix 1 Prolife Passages in the Bible *143*

Appendix 2 Empirical Proof: A Decade of GRTL Political
                and Legislative Evidence *147*

Appendix 3 Online Personhood Resources *153*

Endnotes *155*

Acknowledgments *171*

Index *173*

Preface

June 28, 1992. The phone rang. As I lifted the receiver, I knew the tranquility of my Sunday afternoon was about to be shattered and that my life would never be the same again.

"Daniel Becker?" queried the caller in a calm and matter-of-fact manner.

Timidly and with a fleeting desire to deny the fact, I answered "Yes."

What followed next was an unending stream of colorful profanity.

Having worked in construction for over a decade, I was accustomed to rough language in the workplace, but this experience was different. After twenty seconds of increasing volume and fouler speech, the caller realized I was still listening. No longer content to spew filth and depraved suggestions, he called down curses upon my family and me.

To say that this was your typical obscene phone call, desecrating the sanctity of your home and defiling your spirit—was not exactly true; it was an expected call. In fact, anticipating just such a call I had asked my five teenage children to go upstairs to spare them the memory of seeing their father engaged in conversation with an out-of-control caller whose sole purpose was to vent his emotions in a vile and demonic manner.

Remembering that obscene callers are "persons" too, I waited for the indecent tirade to subside long enough for me to attempt to pierce the emotional attack and try to find "common ground" with the "person" behind the invective mask. It became clear after several minutes of attempting to steer this raw emotional display to a place of reasoned dialogue that I was not going to succeed. Acknowledging defeat, I slowly lowered the phone to its cradle.

Immediately the phone began anew its loud and insistent ringing. I answered this time with an introductory declaration, "Daniel Becker speaking."

"@#%$%!" and then a loud hang-up.

I fielded one call after another—each exactly like the first. I must say that I underestimated the degree to which a raw and wounded humanity, stripped of basic civility, could affect my imperfectly sanctified soul. My Will was determined to take call after call for as long as the phone continued to ring; my Mind was prepared to reason and engage in dialogue and even debate, but my Emotions were wholly unprepared for the demonic onslaught that ensued. My Spirit, rooted in a firm faith in Christ as my Savior and King, slowly began to crumble under the incessant verbal stream of fallen humanity's attack against my family, my faith and my person.

With a heaviness of heart, I answered the next call, "Daniel Becker speaking."

A calm and measured voice inquired, "You live at 1862 Liberty Grove Road?"

At last—an emotionally stable and quiet tone of voice bringing with it the hope of a reasoned conversation.

"Yes," was my muted reply.

He stated his name, going on, "I am a former Navy SEAL. I have seen a picture of you and your family in the news. You have three beautiful daughters. I am coming to rape them and then kill you! . . . @#%$%$ . . . because of what you just did to MY family!!"

I remember the day well...a lazy summer Sunday in rural north Georgia, a day away from my 40th birthday. I was looking forward to getting away to spend quality time with my family. The TV from upstairs blared with the screaming of a crowd as the Atlanta Braves baseball team swept into the pennant lead for the first time in nearly two decades. Millions of viewers all over the nation watched "America's team" as its players defeated their opponent to take over the lead in their division. Indeed, 1992 was remembered as the year the Braves clinched the pennant and went on to the World Series, ultimately becoming the first American team in the history of the game to lose to a foreign opponent.[1]

After an interminable period of horrendous verbal assault, I determined that I could stand to take only one more call.

"Daniel Becker," I answered, my strained voice no doubt reflecting my horror at the realization of the scope of the consequences I had just unleashed upon my timid wife and five innocent older children.

Without identifying themselves, and with a momentary pause on the other end, a mother's voice accompanied by her two teenage daughters began singing the first stanza of a familiar childhood hymn:

Standing by a purpose true,
Heeding God's command,
Honor them, the faithful few!
All hail to Daniel's band!

Many giants, great and tall,
Stalking through the land,
Headlong to the earth would fall,
If met by Daniel's band.

Dare to be a Daniel,
Dare to stand alone!
Dare to have a purpose firm!
Dare to make it known.

Through the tears coursing down my cheeks, I thanked this homeschooling family for reminding me I was not alone. This battle for the "hearts and minds" of Georgia's citizens was going to be monumental in its intensity—that was to be expected; that Christ

Jesus was with me and that ultimately "the battle is the Lord's"—
that was a promise!

And what a battle it was. This simple children's tune reminded
me that the church is *not* walled up defensively within some spiritual
fortress, attempting to defend our lives from the demonic hordes
that are assaulting our families and threatening to rape and pillage
our homes. The situation *is* like that of David—a simple shepherd,
advancing upon a powerfully equipped enemy with nothing more
than the "Name of the Lord" on his lips and armed with five smooth
stones—taking aim at a giant he could not conceivably miss!

The nature of our struggle is revealed by our Lord's proclamation
in the original charter of the church (Matthew 16:18), His
declaration that the church is an offensive force that no power—
not even the "gates of Hell"— can stand against. Gates, as many
have pointed out, are a defensive structure rather than a weapon of
offense; as such they provide us with a strategy for exploiting our
enemies' greatest strength. The "gates" of ignorance and deception
are destroyed whenever we promote the Truth. In reality, it is God's
people who are on the march, going forth to battle for the hearts,
minds and souls of humankind. We advance the gospel into worldly
strongholds.

In Luke 16:16, Jesus points to this invading nature of our role in
getting out "the good news of the kingdom of God." He says it "is
preached and *everyone forces his way into it*" (emphasis added). And
the apostle Paul declares in Romans 8:37 that "in all these things we
are more than conquerors through him who loved us." Conquerors
are intent on only one thing . . . conquest.

Finally I took the phone off the hook.

"How did I get here?" my agonized thoughts shouted. "And
what have I done to my family?"

It only got worse. What I had done that day resulted in my name
and picture appearing on the front page of the Atlanta newspaper for

a record-setting five days in a row. Over the next few weeks, I would become the brunt of editorial cartoonists around the nation. Had I really counted the cost? Torn by doubt, a feeling of despair settled in my heart. Nor did those doubts abate; instead, they reasserted themselves again and again as over the course of the next several months I appeared on numerous national shows: National Public Radio, *Good Morning America*, CNN's *Catherine Cryer Program*; I even received a call from the producer of a new TV show featuring Rush Limbaugh. At the conclusion of an interview on NBC's *The Today Show* with Byrant Gumbel, my microphone was muted as he called for civil rights attorneys around the nation to file suit against me for the "psychological harm" that I had done to children.

This period of intense activity culminated in an onscreen debate with the feminist icon Margie Pitt Hames. Ms. Hames was a national board member for the ACLU and the attorney who had successfully argued the Doe v. Bolton case before the Supreme Court. This case, originating from Georgia, had given our nation abortion-on-demand through all nine months of pregnancy—for any and all reasons. This confrontation with Ms. Hames constituted for me a "supremely" unfair match-up; a carpenter by trade, at best a successful business owner and elder in a local church, arguing against one of the most renowned feminists of her time—I truly felt by this point like David fighting a new "giant" every other week.

As a youth I had been extremely shy, and I had bumbled as a public speaker during my days in Bible college. To this day I continue to struggle to communicate before a crowd. Personally, it was excruciatingly painful for me to stand in the public eye day after day and to take all the abuse a hostile press commands, yet the Lord's grace was always present and sufficient.

Six weeks later my "actions" had generated a court case that is still being reviewed in the law schools of our land.[2] A bit of additional background will help set the scene: One Thursday afternoon, as a candidate for the U.S. Congress, I filed for injunctive relief, appealing an adverse federal court ruling that had chilled my first amendment rights of free speech. Three days later, on a crisp Sunday morning in October, my emergency request found its way to the desk of Supreme Court Justice Anthony Kennedy. After viewing a short video presentation, he refused my request to overturn the lower court ruling. Thus I became the nation's first federal candidate for public office to have my Constitutionally-protected free speech censored by a federal court order "using prior restraint."[3]

This was heady stuff for a former carpenter. What kind of action, you ask, could have precipitated such an unprecedented assault on our nation's basic Constitutional right of "free speech"? Would you believe it had all started with Sunday sports and politics?

Using my Constitutionally-protected status as a federal candidate for the U.S. House of Representatives, I purchased a 30-second advertising spot during an Atlanta Braves game to air what has proven to be the second most common surgical procedure in the United States other than tooth extraction—I aired first- and second-trimester abortions.

Using a collage of clips from a prolife video produced by Gregg Cunningham, I used my federal candidacy to portray the gruesome reality behind the culturally acceptable terms of "choice" and "right to privacy." Suddenly, as a severed head was shown being removed from the "birth canal," we were no longer debating "my body, my right." The rhetoric surrounding abortion was stripped away, and the raw truth that abortion takes the life of a small child was graphically fixed in the consciousness of an audience of over five million viewers.[4] I agreed with prolife crusader Gregg Cunningham that if America is to reject abortion it must first see abortion.

June 28, 1992—Sunday afternoon baseball in the Deep South, a sacrosanct Southern institution . . . and I had just publicly desecrated our local gods and sports deities. The frenzied crowds were calling for my head. Unlike the apostle Paul, who endured an onslaught of actual rocks and stones as a result of standing against the pagan idolatry of his day, I was grateful that for the most part only ridicule, foul abuse and threats were being lobbed in my direction.

November 3, 1992, was the day incumbent president George Bush was defeated by Democratic proabortion candidate Bill Clinton. I also lost to my proabortion Democratic opponent. The truly interesting fact about my loss, though, was that the political pundits (both liberal and conservative) were predicting an absolute rout; instead, the citizens of Georgia's 9th U.S. House District awarded me the largest vote for a Republican in the district's history. Unfortunately, a Republican had not been elected in the district in since Reconstruction.

Three years later my opponent switched parties and became a Republican—the first Republican House member in modern times to represent this area of north Georgia. Today, eighteen years later, he is the governor of Georgia[5] and solidly prolife, holding a no-exception[6] position on abortion and calling for a personhood amendment to our state constitution! Additionally, Georgia's 9th District is known as the most solidly prolife U.S. House district in the state. Instead of going down in flames for my bold, imprudent and unapologetic defense of innocent human life, my race was living testimony, to the political powers, that a candidate can do well in the political arena and compete in the marketplace of public policy while running with a bold prolife emphasis.

Opponents to Personhood strategy say that this "all or nothing" approach is ill-advised. They love to point out that "Losing is *not* costless." On the contrary, a loss is not detrimental if it inspires others to follow your lead, mobilizes the troops, engages public debate and lays the foundation for future political action. My loss laid the foundation for an unbroken string of victories and prolife advances over the next decade. One such victory was my former campaign aide, Martin Scott, who ran successfully for the Georgia House and later introduced the nation's first Personhood amendment to a state legislature.

My 1992 campaign director is the newly elected Public Service Commissioner for our state,[7] in 2008 he ran the Personhood effort for Georgia Right to Life. Nearly all of the major prolife political advances have come from Georgia's 9th District; the offices of governor and lieutenant governor are currently held by prolife individuals, and the ranks of the prolife officials also include our caucus leader and most of our core politicians. Most of our prolife legislation has been sponsored by an incumbent from the 9th U.S. House District, and our current 9th District congressman, Tom Graves, is the husband of a former chapter leader for Georgia Right to Life.

In the aftermath of my defeat, and on the basis of my clear public stand against the horror of abortion, I was asked to serve as Political Action Committee (PAC) Director for Georgia Right to Life, a post I held for eight years. Those were years of conflict and change. I am especially grateful to the past president of GRTL, Caryl Swift, for embracing and working for a biblical reexamination of our goals and objectives, along with a strategy to best accomplish them. She was always gracious and supportive of my requests to reconsider our actions in light of God's Word and His ways. She more than anyone else deserves the credit for the accomplishments of the last decade, as she demonstrated the calm and gracious spirit of Christ to all with whom she came into contact—friend and foe alike. Her example inspired all of us to labor "by the strength that God supplies" (1 Peter 4:11), and she and the entire staff deserve the credit for the tremendous advance of the prolife agenda in Georgia.

The first change I requested as PAC director was to our endorsement criteria. I asked for and received permission from our board of directors to change the basis for determining whether a politician or candidate was considered to be "prolife." No longer was "rape and incest" an acceptable position for being welcomed into the prolife camp and endorsed by our organization. Michigan and Tennessee being the only other NRLC state affiliates in the nation holding the same policy, we joined forces with Michigan Right to Life and began to see some of the same victories they had achieved. In fact, it was largely due to the Michigan organization's incredible political and legislative successes with the position that our own "moderates" were won over by the argument of sheer pragmatism.

To declare that "all hell broke loose" politically would be a huge understatement. As a matter of fact, our actions proved highly unpopular with friend and foe alike. Almost half of our board members resigned over the next few months, and our own pro-family and prolife allies castigated our decision and expelled us from their inner circle; their access to power was jeopardized by being aligned too closely with what the local press was labeling "an extremist organization."

The second change we implemented was also a significant departure from the norm: It was decided that our PAC would not operate from the position of being a "kingmaker," a paradigm after which so many other pro-family groups are modeled. Instead we would present ourselves as "standard bearers," our sole responsibility being to uphold and enforce a consistent biblical standard that would protect all innocent human life. We rejected political compromise, currying favor and other "quid pro quo" activities and became an impartial judge of friend and foe alike. Either you as a candidate held a truly prolife position or you did not get our endorsement. This applied to seasoned "prolife" incumbents as well as to newcomers on the scene. The outcry of objections from within the entrenched camp of "prolife" incumbents was the loudest.

Over the next decade we saw politicians of all stripes "convert" their former "rape and incest" exceptions to a pure no-exception position.[8] At the present time fifty-five percent (55%) of our

Georgia Senate holds a "no exception" position, including our governor, lieutenant governor, attorney general and the individuals holding six other statewide offices, not to mention a majority of our U.S. Representatives. We have passed most of the prolife legislation recommended by the national Right to Life groups. Ten years ago we had no effectual prolife legislation, but since we raised the level of the bar to require a biblical standard of our politicians our ranking has risen from among the least prolife states to the eighth most prolife state in the nation in 2010.[9]

Little could I imagine that the chain of events that began that summer in 1992 would allow me, by God's grace, and in a small way, to contribute to a national Personhood movement, changing the way we as a nation view prolife efforts in the 21st century.

This book attempts to define and answer many of the questions being asked by prolife activists and supporters today concerning Personhood: What is it? Why is it necessary? Can the strategy win? Is the timing right? How can I start a movement in my state?

I trust that you will find this book to be a useful contribution to the dialogue.

Chapter 1

Personhood, Prudence, and Pragmatism, Without Compromise

The Struggle to Be Prolife in the 21st Century

It has been nearly forty years since abortion was legalized in the United States through all nine months of pregnancy . . . for any and all reasons. Over 53 million children have died, and their parents have been scarred by either regret or callousness. Two generations of young people have grown to adulthood during those years, never knowing a time when law protected the preborn and criminalized a doctor for aiding a mother in taking the life of her own child. In the intervening years, respect and protection for human life of all ages has eroded to the point that Princeton University accords Peter Singer a prestigious endowed chair in Bioethics. Dr. Singer is torn between advocating for the death of his senile mother (Alzheimer patient) because she has ceased to be a "person" and the duty of a son to care for his aging parent.[10] "He did state that if he were solely responsible [*if his sister had no say in the matter*], his mother might not be alive today."[11]

In the same argument, he posits "if perfectly normal toddlers were to be killed by their parents, it would not be as grave an evil as killing a 'person.' Moreover, although a normal newborn baby has no sense of the future, and therefore is not a *person* [italics mine], that does not mean that it is all right to kill such a baby. It only means that the wrong done to the infant is not as great as the wrong that would be done to a *person* [italics mine] who was killed."[12]

The assault on human dignity and the sanctity of life continues on another front—that of human-animal hybrids (chimeras). In May 2008 Cornell University combined the "glow-in-the-dark" genes of an Australian jellyfish with those of a child at the embryonic stage of life. The resultant chimera was a scientific "success." But the creature that was part human child and part animal died when the research was completed. Even to many secular observers this elicits a visceral response of moral repugnance. But the overriding, operative question is whether this form of research is legal in the US. A recent *New York Times* article reports that "A spokesman for the National Institutes of Health said the Cornell work would not be classified as gene therapy in need of federal review, because a test-tube embryo is not considered a *person* [italics mine] under the regulations."[13] In other words, federal regulations fail to restrain this moral evil because the embryo "is not considered a *person*" under the U.S. Constitution. Abortion, euthanasia, destructive stem cell research, human-animal hybrids and cloning—the question of "Personhood" is at the center of every one of these assaults on human life and dignity.

Having failed to stop abortion in the 20th Century, we are now experiencing the long-prophesied "slippery slope" effect—the assault on innocent life by means of emerging technology supported by uninformed public sentiment, unrestrained by moral absolutes. The battleground for the sanctity of life in the 21st Century has moved well beyond abortion. Major biotech research labs at our universities routinely kill children at an embryonic level through using unethical research methods, and are now allied with the old abortion lobby against human dignity. Big biotech companies and many public policy advocates now use the terms "cure" or "therapy" to justify their evil work before an adoring public. Many Americans have replaced their trust in Almighty God and are now worshiping at the altar of Technology. The future indeed appears bleak.

Add to this the frustration felt by the vast majority of younger prolife advocates whose unanswered questions are "Why did our parents' generation fail to stop abortion? After all, it has been four decades! Where did they go wrong?" "Did they go wrong?" "Why haven't we been able to outlaw this evil?" These are fair questions. Frustrated and incensed, these younger prolife supporters are openly questioning the current direction of the movement. One of our homegrown southern sages states it this way, "If we do what we always did, then we get what we always got . . . nothing." This frustration has resulted in the wholesale endorsement of Personhood as a legal and public policy objective among a new generation of prolife ministries.[14] Many in the younger generation are questioning the long-standing prolife strategy of seeking legal limitation and regulation of abortion; instead they are actively engaged in promoting the larger issue of Personhood, which encompasses much more than this singular evil. As paraplegic Joni Erikson Tada warns us, "this is a season, perhaps, like none other, to truly influence the world— we must safeguard the Personhood of all human beings, for if we do not, then the infant with severe mental retardation will be labeled a 'pre-person,' and the young man with profound brain injury will be labeled a 'non-person,' and Mr. and Mrs. Hill (Alzheimer's patients), in a few years . . . will be labeled 'post-persons.'"[15]

In themselves, emotions of fear, worry, and frustration are a poor basis for developing a victorious prolife strategy in the 21st Century. We must demonstrate a principled, prudent, yet pragmatic approach that produces the desired results—a recognition from within the culture and embodied in our law that all innocent human life should be protected. Embracing the centuries-old objective and strategy of Personhood is what I purport will accomplish these goals.

Personhood Defined

What is Personhood? It is the recognition by our culture and our government that each individual human life has an "unalienable" right to life from its earliest biological beginning. This right to life extends to natural death, regardless of one's disability, gender, race, dependency or manner of conception. The "unalienable" right to life comes from God by virtue of the fact, that we have been created in His image and are thus imbued with a unique worth and dignity not found in the rest of creation.

My purpose in writing this book is to share with prolife advocates the remarkable success we have experienced in the state of Georgia over the last decade as we stood firmly upon the policy of Personhood. We have accomplished this by promoting a culture of life that is primarily reflected within the culture, is mirrored in political success, and has resulted in Georgia being recognized by other national prolife ministries as one of the leading states in terms of the volume of prolife legislation that has been enacted.

Here are a few empirical facts to be considered: A short ten years ago Georgia had no effectual prolife laws on the books[16], and only 3% of our legislators claimed to be prolife without exceptions. My organization, Georgia Right to Life, was labeled by the local media as being an "extremist group" due to our rigid definition of what constitutes a "prolife " candidate. Contrast that with the situation today: Georgia voters, both Democratic (72%) and Republican (75%), have expressed their support of a Personhood amendment to the Georgia constitution.[17] In the November 2010 elections, every statewide constitutional office in Georgia (Governor, Lieutenant Governor, Attorney General, etc.—nine in total) was won by a prolife official who signed his support of a Personhood amendment to the state constitution. Each personally holds that abortion should be illegal except in cases where the mother's life is in danger *and* only after both the mother and the child have been treated equally when attempting to preserve life (no exceptions).[18] The majority of the members of our Georgia Senate also claimed a "no exceptions" position on abortion, while 40% of the Georgia House does. (In

2000, that number was less than 3%.) The number rises to 50% if members who advocate rape and incest exception are included. Most of the prolife laws suggested by national groups have been enacted; we are ranked eighth in this regard.

Promoting Personhood has not only been successful in Georgia but has, in many ways, challenged the status quo of our nation's current prolife movement.

Ten years ago, I had a conversation with a national prolife leader. He warned that if we insisted on pursuing this objective, we would be responsible for setting back the prolife movement in Georgia. We would alienate our prolife legislators, marginalize our organization politically and culturally, and that we would be called "extremist" by the press. Finally, he warned that our prolife allies would abandon us. While several of his predictions did come about, we cannot be accused of undermining the achievement of our objectives. We are impacting the culture, achieving legislative victories, and continuing to elect prolife office holders.

One example of cultural impact is our ranking in calls into pregnancy resource centers. For six years in a row according to CareNet, Georgia has recorded more calls to crisis pregnancy centers than has any other state in the nation. Hearts and minds are being changed; lives are being saved. We are also seeing increasing awareness and activity in the African American community and historically black colleges and universities.

How does one measure success in our prolife calling if not in terms of the hearts and minds that have been changed and the resultant lives that have been saved? Our per capita abortions have dropped dramatically over the last ten years.

I firmly believe that the predominant prolife movement failed to achieve its desired legal, political, and cultural objectives when it abandoned Personhood as a strategy in the late 1970's. Priorities were inverted by first seeking the overturn of Roe v. Wade, rather than by tackling the more difficult task of shifting public opinion in favor of the sanctity of life. Our nation's experience of Prohibition should have taught us that the legal objective can never precede public opinion. We might pass laws that enforce our goals, but, lacking public support, they are destined to fall.

Additionally, overturning Roe should never have become the first objective, because it quickly led to compromise of principle. The principal message that all innocent human life should be protected regardless of circumstances of conception was prostituted at the ballot box. Lawmakers were not required to embrace the sanctity of life as an inviolable component of their moral compasses. They proclaimed themselves "prolife" but when faced with tough decisions, they abandoned life issues in favor of immediate political gain. This is not prudence, as some proclaim. This is that for which Congressman Stupak and others were punished in the 2010 election cycle; it is compromise.

Past compromises by prolife lawmakers introduced "exceptions" in which they agreed that a child could be put to death based on its manner of conception. In 1977 prolife leaders capitulated to political pressure and agreed to allow, for the first time, for a narrow class of humans to be legally killed by abortion. The Hyde Amendment, the vehicle that introduced these "exceptions," was defended as moral by saying, in essence, that "we must do evil that good may come." The intent was to save lives, an objective that was no doubt accomplished through the outlawing of federal funding for abortion; nonetheless, the immediate result was that our principled objective of Personhood was severely damaged.

Was this damage necessary in order to save lives? Not in my opinion. I believe the case could be made that our justification on the grounds of "saving lives" actually cost us many more! In Georgia, we have experienced the same challenge from our respected prolife leaders who have repeatedly asked us to allow "rape and incest" exceptions to be added to a critical prolife bill. They assure us that the bill is dead unless we lower our standards and succumb to political pressure. In every case we refused. Since adopting the Personhood strategy Georgia has passed a substantial amount of prolife law and we have managed to save 100% of the babies . . . not the 98.5% the rest of the movement allows. More importantly, we preserve the principle of Personhood so that the foundational premise of the sanctity of all life is upheld.

The Hyde Amendment damaged the very fabric of our mission. No longer would the lofty rhetoric of "sanctity of all human life" and "the personhood of the unborn" be embodied in a strategy to achieve those protections. The prolife movement had a seat at the political table, but contented itself with crumbs. For the next thirty years, "prolife" presidents and "prolife" Senate and House majorities came and went, while the movement was directed to be patient and not "rock the boat." The resignation by the movement was verbalized: "After all, what more can we expect in a fallen world?" In the ensuing years, over 53 million children died and the battleground expanded exponentially. That is a terrible price to pay for untethering our strategy from our foundational principle.

I believe that we can and should expect more! We should plan for victory by correctly identifying our objectives and prioritizing our actions to accomplish a successful strategy. We accomplished this in Georgia by reaffirming the biblical premise of Personhood. We then educated our base of supporters and our politicians. After that we notified all candidates, including the few "prolife" incumbents, that we would no longer accept compromise of the basic life principles. Over time, this resulted in the election of truly prolife legislators. For every one elected, ten others were influenced.

Of the many prolife laws that have been passed in Georgia over the last ten years, the state has not enacted a single piece of legislation that includes rape and incest exceptions for abortion. We are the first state in the nation whose voters have approved Personhood as a constitutional objective, albeit through a non-binding poll. All of this has arguably changed the entire political landscape in Georgia. It was clearly admitted to me by a former leader in the Democratic party that one cannot get elected statewide in Georgia unless he or she is prolife. This has led to our proabortion opponents alluding to Georgia Right to Life as the "shadow government of Georgia." As flattering as this sounds, we certainly do not make this claim.

While we still have a way to go before we can declare victory, no one can deny that pursuing Personhood has been a most successful strategy. It has produced a documented shift in public opinion, success in the area of political action and the enactment of prolife legislation.

I have saved my strongest argument for last: Personhood is biblical! As such, it opposes worldly wisdom—it is, after all, otherworldly in origin. The apostle Paul has written that, while "having the appearance of godliness" worldly wisdom denies its power, becoming reprobate as concerns the faith (2 Timothy 3:5). God's revealed truth must always be the ground of our faith, not reason. Our minds must always be subject to His Spirit. That is not to say that our faith is anti-reason. Faith is as "reasonable" as its object is. What could be more trustworthy in this respect than placing our faith in Almighty God, the Creator and Sustainer of all life, and trusting in the power of faithful obedience to His Word?

From the Middle Ages onward, the Church has struggled with the revival of paganism and its primary prophets: Cicero, Seneca, Plato and Aristotle. The Renaissance tempted the Church to abandon its foundational faith in the veracity of God's revelation, adding to it man's wisdom and thereby producing a syncretism devoid of power. This is the key distinction between the current national prolife vision and the Georgia vision. The former strategy claims the authority of reasonableness, as taught by Aristotle. The other relies upon the trustworthiness of God's revealed will and ways, as taught in the Bible, His word.[20]

In the summer of 1973 I studied briefly at L'Abri Fellowship with Dr. Francis Schaeffer, who was fond of saying that the Bible is true truth but not exhaustive truth. God's Word is completely truthful about everything to which it speaks, but it does not speak to or about everything there is to know. I am not opposed to extra-biblical knowledge, wisdom, or prudence; the Bible itself is full of examples in which the biblical authors cite external sources of wisdom or knowledge. Nor do I dispute using extra-biblical truth as a guide, but I do contest its use as an authority and a de facto justification of moral cowardice and reductionist orthopraxy. I am especially disturbed when the revelation of God and His ways is supplanted by lofty human reason masquerading as godly wisdom.

Mother Teresa has stated that God has not called us to success but rather to faithfulness. The modern prolife movement should sit at her feet.

Summary

It is not often that one hears the concept of faithfulness discussed as part of our promotion of prolife goals and strategy. But it has been by God's grace and power, poured out on our often feeble attempts to be found faithful before Him, that His truth has triumphed to the extent that it has manifested itself in our state.

Others have sought a more "reasonable" explanation by stating that these victories have come about as a result of our funding or organizational skills. While it is true that we have sought to be good stewards of God's gifts and abilities, ask anyone who has contributed over the last decade and they will cite example after miraculous example of God's providential dealings that have caused our enemies to flee and His truth to be ensconced in the hearts of people and the laws of our state. To God alone be the glory! It is only as we repent of our dependence upon human wisdom and confess our need of God that we can expect Him to show Himself strong on our behalf—and that we will see prolife victory in the 21st century.

Chapter 2

Personhood: Roadmap to Victory

If you don't know where you are going, any road will get
you there.

Lewis Carroll

Thus says the LORD: "Stand by the roads, and look, and ask
for the ancient paths, where the good way is; and walk in it,
and find rest for your souls." But they said, "We will not walk
in it."

Jeremiah 6:16

"Where are we nearly four decades after Roe v. Wade? And
how did we get here? 53 million plus dead! What went wrong?"
These questions are just a sampling of the ones being asked by third
generation prolifers. Largely younger and more active than their
parents before them, today's activists want more action and fewer
excuses for a lack of victories on the prolife front. Typically they have
the drive and enthusiasm of youth, but lack any clear trumpet call-
to-arms from the "troopers" who have gone before them. What they
hear instead is "Wait until we capture the Senate and can appoint
Supreme Court Justices," "Wait until the timing on the Court is
right," "Wait, wait, wait . . . !"

Dr. Martin Luther King Jr., writing from the Birmingham jail,
replied as follows to those timid souls in the civil rights movement who
were cautioning him that his actions were "unwise and untimely":

"For years now I have heard the word 'Wait!' It rings in the ear of every Negro with piercing familiarity. This 'Wait' has almost always meant 'Never.' We must come to see, with one of our distinguished jurists, that 'justice too long delayed is justice denied.'"[21]

The children of Israel had to wait for 40 years while wandering in their wilderness of inaction; must the same be true for the prolife movement in the 21st century? It is clear to many, especially in the younger generation, that the prolife movement has lost its way.

When one is lost, the surest way to get out of the wilderness is to consult your compass (today your GPS) and compare it with a trusted map. This will not only tell you where you are going but will reveal the point at which you stepped off the path to begin with. A hiker can spend a lot of money on a highly accurate GPS, but without a correspondingly accurate map embedded in the software, he or she will be no closer to getting home. One would be better off to navigate using the sun and stars than to attempt to cross a wilderness with a compass and an imprecise map scribbled on the inside cover of a pack of matches.

The prolife movement has been placing its trust in a map that does not lead home. Since the early 1970's the movement has been split over which map to follow—legal protections for human life as defined by government or Personhood as defined by God and recognized by government. While both segments of the movement agree that divine law dictates its policy objectives, the "official" branch claims natural law[22] as its authority for its strategy and the other branch bases its strategy in divine law.[23]

Personhood as a Policy Objective

From its inception in 1974 National Right to Life Committee (NRLC) set out to impact public opinion and enact a human life amendment (HLA) at a federal level. Most prolife groups throughout the last four decades have shared this policy objective. Dr. Jack

Willke, past president of NRLC, published this objective on page 3 of his landmark prolife book titled *Abortion: Questions and Answers*: "The ultimate prolife goal is quite direct and simple. Prolifers want an amendment to the U.S. Constitution, to the Canadian Charter of Rights that will give equal protection under the law, to all living humans from the time their biologic life begins at fertilization until natural death." He went on to add that "Understanding that such a goal [Federal HLA] remains yet in the future, prolife people have an intermediate goal . . . returning the right to make decisions about abortion to each individual state . . . ."

To return the right to ban abortion at a state level would require the reversal or nullification of the 1973 ruling of Roe v. Wade. There are a number of ways that the movement envisions this being accomplished, and strategy, not policy, is where the current debate stands. Prolife activists around the country are once again debating state level Personhood as a strategy.

Personhood as a Strategy

Only "persons" are recognized as having legal standing under our federal and state constitutions, a reality that requires the term "person" to be constitutionally defined to include all classes of human life, regardless of dependency or disabilities—which of course would include the preborn. This has led many prolife leaders to reject Personhood as unobtainable strategically, citing the current makeup of the courts as being unfavorable. The objection, they claim, is that the courts will not support the legal protection of human life by *governmental definition*. I agree that they are probably correct in this assessment. They fail to discern that this is not what we are asking our lawmakers or judges to do, we are demanding the *legal recognition* by government of Personhood.

This difference may appear small and nuanced, but the ramifications are immense. Government cannot be allowed the prerogative of claiming to define a right that has never been within its rightful jurisdiction. The right to life comes from God, not government. Personhood is the human rights movement of the 21st century, not an attorney's playground. Our prolife policy objectives, strategies and corporate actions should always acknowledge this important fact. The current Personhood debate centers, in substance, around whose authority will direct our course . . . prudential human reason based upon natural law or prudential human reason based upon divine law.

A Short History

Burke Balch is a National Right to Life (NRLC) board member and the director of the Robert Powell Center for Medical Ethics. While speaking at the 2009 NRLC national convention on the history of the modern prolife movement, he told the audience that the movement, over the last four decades, has split no less than three times over the issue of Personhood.

The first split was in the early 1970's, when NRLC board member Nellie Gray challenged the movement to reject compromise within the ranks. She specifically took issue with "rape and incest" exceptions being granted to otherwise "prolife" candidates, also objecting to these "exceptions" being included in the legislation they sponsored. Her battle cry was "NO EXCEPTION! NO COMPROMISE!" She was accused of moral perfectionism by the prolife leadership, and her admonition was rejected on the grounds that the "greater good" must be sacrificed in order to achieve a "lesser good." The authority for this strategy, they claim, is based upon Greek philosopher Aristotle's position on the four virtues of prudence, justice, courage and temperance.[24] Additionally, these leaders frequently quote the godless French philosopher Voltaire's precept, "The best is the enemy of the good."[25]

In response, Nellie Gray established guidelines for the movement, known as "Life Principles," which state their immediate objective as follows: "WHEREFORE, Pursuant To These Principles, we recommend and urge the adoption of a Mandatory HUMAN LIFE AMENDMENT to the Constitution of the United States of America." When her appeal for no compromise failed, she resigned from the NRLC board and founded the annual March for Life in Washington, D.C. Each year for nearly four decades these Life Principles are read to those gathered on the mall in Washington, D.C. Many prolifers view Nellie Grey as the grandame of Personhood.

The second split occurred when former NRLC board member Judie Brown left NRLC to found the American Life League in 1979. Once again the movement was confronted by its willingness to give tacit endorsement of abortion in cases of rape and incest to candidates that proclaimed themselves "prolife." Her opposition led her to call for the immediate passage of a human life amendment at either the state or federal level. Her bold witness and strong opposition to compromise within the movement have served as an example and testimony to Truth to many millions of the Catholic faithful. Her organization has often been a lone voice within the Catholic community, challenging Catholic leaders, including members of the powerful U.S. Conference of Catholic Bishops.[26] Her organization claims to be the largest prolife organization in the United States.

The latest split involving Personhood was a result of the nation's first filing of a human life amendment at the state legislative level.[27] On March 20, 2007, NRLC affiliate Georgia Right to Life sponsored a House resolution (H.R. 536)[28] calling for a paramount human life amendment to the Georgia constitution. Representative Martin Scott, a leading member of the prolife caucus, was its author. It was followed a few months later by a ballot initiative in Colorado led by a home-schooled woman named Kristi Burton. Both attempts failed in their respective states but succeeded in igniting a national awareness of Personhood and a refocusing of the movement on the biblical imperative. In 2008 Keith Mason and Cal Zastrow founded a national organization, PersonhoodUSA, to coordinate citizen-led ballot initiatives.

Those of us pursuing Personhood as a strategy do not disagree with national leaders on policy objectives; the issue is which strategy to employ to achieve them. In all three cases the current leadership of the prolife movement was challenged to reconsider Personhood as a strategy from a biblical perspective, based on divine law. In each case the movement responded by rejecting the admonition and embracing a course of strategy based upon natural law.

Divine Law v. Natural Law

A remarkable sight greets a visitor to main chamber of the Supreme Court of the United States. The very first thing the Justices see as they are seated at the Bench, on the west wall of the courtroom, is a frieze by acclaimed classical sculptor Adolph A. Weinman (1870–1952). He allegorically portrays God's immutable attribute of "Justice" holding a sword as the central concept of the frieze. To the right of Justice is "Divine Inspiration". "'Justice' faces to the viewer's right, staring down the forces of Evil. The winged figure of *Divine Inspiration* holds out the *Scales of Justice*. Flanking these two figures are representations of *Wisdom*, to the left, with an owl perched on his shoulder, and *Truth*, to the right, holding a mirror and a rose."[29] Does it come as a surprise to you that our highest court acknowledges the centrality of God's word as the foundational element of our concept of Justice . . . that Wisdom and Truth originate from this pairing? If our Supreme Court acknowledges this fact, then why do we not see more mention of God and His ways among the leadership of the prolife movement?

As I see it, herein lies the dividing issue: Which system of law will our movement follow; and, if both are required, are both of equal weight and authority? The apostle Paul, in Romans 2:14-16, indicated that there are two sources of law: one by means of special revelation (divine law) and the other supplied by conscience (natural law).[30]

I believe that the classical teaching on natural law and divine law has been corrupted by specious reasonings and faulty application as it applies to the strategy of the prolife movement. My unorthodox definitions are my feeble attempt to highlight the serious departure from the true path to prolife victory based on a firm conviction that God is responsive to our faith, our prayers and our faithfulness.

The Judeo-Christian concept of divine law purports that God has revealed an absolute truth—that all innocent human life bears His image and hence has immense worth and value; this is my understanding of the sanctity of life and more specifically, Personhood. The proper exercise of justice demands that our court apply this divine inspiration to assure protection for the preborn. Most Christians do not believe that it is within the jurisdiction of government to define who is and who is not a person. Our founding fathers declared this when they stated that our right to life comes from our Creator God.[31] This right is innate and inalienable. We would never derive this truth by the natural law alone. Natural law must be informed by divine revelation. Twenty year old, founding father Alexander Hamilton, admits as much in his pamphlet entitled *The Farmer Refuted*. In defining the "laws of nature" he emphatically states, "The Sacred Rights of Mankind are not to be rummaged for, among old parchments, or musty records. They are written with a sun beam, in the whole volume of human nature, by the Hand of the Divinity itself; and can never be erased or obscured by mortal power."

Natural law, as asserted today by many prolife leaders, draws its authority on a presumed absolute demanded by Reason and supposedly shared by all humans,[32] not on a moral absolute whose authority is God the Creator. I agree that natural law finds its genesis in divine law since all morality originates with the character and attributes of Almighty God, yet it is clear that natural law as a sole authority is corrupted by fallen human nature. This corruption is manifest in the way some prolife leaders pragmatically discount God's commands and elevate natural law to a supreme and paramount position. Catholic theologian Thomas Aquinas in his *Treatise on Law* frames the issue in this light, "Human law has the nature of law in so far as it partakes of right reason; and it is clear that, in this respect, it is derived from the eternal law. But in so far as it deviates from reason, it is called an unjust law, and has the nature, not of law but of violence." Thus, the "right reason" of human law, according to Aquinas, derives from and cannot conflict with God's law. For when it does, it is no law at all; it is violence. Robert Muise, attorney for Thomas More Law Center says, "Consequently, properly understood, legalized abortion is violence and can never be justified as an acceptable 'law'." Divine laws states that a child must not be put to death for the crimes of its father (Deuteronomy 24:16). To turn a blind eye to this command for the sake of temporal political gain is violence to a revealed truth from God's word.

True Christian belief must require that divine law rule over natural law and our founding fathers agreed. The two are NOT equal, even though BOTH were acknowledged in our Declaration of Independence[33] and BOTH are to be consulted when crafting law. Commenting on natural law and divine law, William Blackstone, author of *Lex Rex* (Latin: the Law is King) explained, "Upon these two foundations, the law of nature and the law of revelation, depend all human laws." Harry V. Jaffa, Professor of Government at Claremont Graduate School and respected authority on our nation's founding principles, argues that America is the first regime in Western history to co-join the claims of Revelation and Reason.[34]

"The tragedy of Western civilization has been the unfettered attempt, by political means, to vindicate claims whose very nature excludes the possibility that they can be vindicated by political means. To attempt to overcome the skepticism that is the ground of philosophy is like trying to jump over one's own shadow. To attempt to remove the necessity of the free and unconstrained faith that is the ground of the Bible and of biblical religion is like denying the existence of the shadow by jumping only in the dark—or with one's eyes shut!"[35]

Ideas have Consequences

I charge that many in prolife leadership, redefine natural law and apply it illicitly. From their perspective, Justice is not based on the immutable character of God, but rather on what good can be accomplished in a "fallen world." Cicero speaks to this view when he declared that "the law is whatever promotes good and forbids evil."[36] This sounds wise until it is applied through the lens of a corrupt, fallen nature. Our own history has shown that governments cannot be entrusted with a legal construct of Personhood based solely on natural law, as this tends toward an arbitrary consensus based on worldly wisdom. This leads to compromise and accommodation to that which divine law forbids, such as, permitting and promoting the killing of children based on their manner of conception. Or in GRTL's recent experience, you have the Georgia Conference of Catholic Bishops testifying before the House Judiciary Committee along side of Planned Parenthood, in opposition to the Human Life Amendment in Georgia. They reasoned that the timing was not right. When asked to defend their action, proponents of this form of action claim the authority of Thomas Aquinas[37], even though law Professor Charles Rice of Notre Dame, author of *50 Questions on the Natural Law* assures me that this is not the teaching or proper application of Aquinas' intent.[38] I am told, that for the Catholic faithful, this is considered scandalous. I would agree.

I have always believed that the enemy of God's best is always *second best*; that *good* is always the enemy of *best*, therefore moralists will always elect to restrict a lesser evil when a greater evil could be completely banned with a little more moral certitude. The law of God clearly commands, "children are not to be put to death for crimes committed by their parents" (Dt 24:16 GNT[39]). This specific command is ignored and violated by those who argue for Aristotelian "prudence" in political discourse and policy, specifically when advocating for "prolife" law that permits rape and incest executions. Rejecting this "prudence" based argument in natural law, *because* it violates divine law, has proven to be of paramount importance when attributing the basis of our success in Georgia politics and public policy.

Two Maps: Two strategies: Two Destinations

The prolife movement is thus torn between following two different "maps." Whether we hold divine law as supreme over natural law will not only determine our prolife objectives but will speak loudly to the strategies necessary to bring about those objectives. It will place limits on our moral participation in evil, rejecting the lie of natural law, which states that at times "we must do evil that good may come," or, as Aristotle put it, "We must as second best . . . take the least of the evils." I agree with our founding father William Penn that "To do evil that good may come of it—is for bunglers in politics as well as morals." If we agree that the sanctity of life comes from God, and that divine law must have paramount authority over natural law, ipso facto, divine law must be our map and guide.

Let's take a look at how history has used these differing maps as a guide—for evil and for good.

Personhood in Antiquity

The concept of Manhood is found throughout the annals of recorded history. It refers to a "coming of age," a reaching of maturity, and the subsequent legal recognition and independence that are granted by the surrounding religious, cultural and governmental entities of the age. Manhood is traditionally associated with physical growth, external accomplishments and gender. To obtain Manhood is to be granted certain rights and corresponding responsibilities. Most pagan cultures developed a sophisticated set of rituals and ceremony to mark the attainment of this stage of male life. Manhood is uniquely male.

This pagan concept of Manhood has produced a literal world of suffering and abuse for humans outside of this clearly recognized "class" of human life. Slaves, captives of war, certain tribes or races, women and those with disabilities and other noticeable weaknesses have all been denied access to the rights and privileges of this class of male elite. This was never God's intent.

Judeo-Christian Construct of Personhood

We find God's plan for personhood in the book of Genesis. God's egalitarian pronouncment of joint Personhood abolishes this exclusive "male only" concept of manhood and expands the concept of mankind to include women. In the words of Genesis 1:27, "So God created man in his own image, in the image of God he created him; male and female he created them." Wherever this foundational precept is embraced, the definition of manhood is transformed from a male-only privilege to mankind [or, in today's terminology, humankind][40]: male and female members of the human race, each equally imbued with a unique imprimatur of God's own likeness and image. Male and female enjoy equal access to God and are charged equally to care for God's creation by means of differing, yet complimentary, roles and responsibilities (Genesis 1–3).

The apostle Paul expanded this notion of equal worth in God's eyes to include *believing* men and women of varying ethnic and social standing; in Galatians 3:28 he says, "There is neither Jew nor Greek, there is neither slave nor free, there is neither male nor female, for you are all one in Christ Jesus."

Judeo-Christian teaching, in contrast to Buddhism or Hinduism, added yet another element to Western culture with the assertion that an individual is comprised of a temporal body and an immortal soul. The immaterial *soul* belongs to the individual human regardless of his or her degree of social status, physical development, dependency or legal standing. The *soul* represents the moral seat of each individual human, and as such God holds each individual human accountable for his or her own volition regarding salvation or damnation. In Christian teaching there is no reincarnation or continuation of successive consciousness; there is instead a single individual existence: "[I]t is appointed for man to die once, and after that comes judgment" (Hebrews 9:27). One could be a serf, a landowner, a ruler or a captive slave in a foreign land, yet each was (and is) responsible equally and individually before God for their moral choices. God will judge each one after this life.

Roman Construct of Personhood

This Judeo-Christian view of law was in stark opposition to the Roman concept of *persona*, which is Latin for *mask*. A *mask* is an external symbol that represents an assumed identity not entirely identical to what lies beneath. In this respect this concept is very similar to the Hebrew notion of *Imago Dei* (Latin: image of God). The difference is that under Roman law Personhood was an artificial legal construct thought to overlay the actual individual—a product of governmental definition. In Roman law a *persona* was a legal entity with all of the privileges and protection of Roman law; as a legal construct Roman law defined those who enjoyed the duties and responsibilities of being a person and proscribed those who did not. A slave was not a *persona* and did not enjoy the protection of law in cases of life, liberty or rights of property—including his or her own children. Under Roman law, then, Personhood was *defined* and applied to some, as opposed to being *recognized* as an inalienable right incarnate in all.

The Victory of Divine Law Over Roman Law

Under the direction of divine law, Christian teaching influenced the Roman culture and by the 4th century had transmuted the Roman concept of *persona* to apply not only to all social classes and genders but to all stages of human life, beginning with the preborn and extending to the elderly infirm.

The Didache (A.D. 95) is one of the earliest extant Christian writings and, though not considered inspired or canonical, is instructive of early Church thought regarding young children— both preborn and born: ". . . do not murder a child by abortion or kill a newborn infant."

By the Middle Ages Western culture based its laws on a biblical understanding of Personhood. Man was created in the image of God and had intrinsic worth and value. In the 6th century Emperor Justinian of Byzantium declared throughout the empire that any live product of a botched abortion or a child found abandoned on the side of the road was to be afforded all of the rights of a freeborn Person. "Without distinction," he decreed, "those who are reared in this way by such persons are to be regarded as free and freeborn *persons*, and they may acquire and dispose of property as they wish, to their own heirs or others, untouched by any taint of servitude or legal subordination or condition of serfdom . . ." Our current Christian understanding of Personhood dates from this time.

Western Law's Construct of Personhood

With the reemergence of a pagan worldview during the Renaissance, explicitly Christian law was joined by a syncretistic mix of pagan Greek scholarship to form the basis of our "common" or Western law. Once again the State presumed to define Personhood and assign the duties, rights, and responsibilities that reside with each citizen. This is in stark opposition to recognizing Personhood as coming from God and inherent in every human in equal measure. Instead of viewing Personhood as an absolute right granted by God, we Westerners see the government stepping in to define and regulate.

Western law's historic struggle over the issue of Personhood is clearly seen in the manner by which the concept has been applied to the issues of slavery, suffrage and eugenics. According to Center for Bio-ethical Reform, "This disturbing pattern of disputing someone's humanity to weaken his claims to rights of Personhood repeats itself again and again in Western history."

In September of 1787 the Constitutional Convention meeting in Philadelphia declared in Article 1, Section 2 of the American Constitution that: "blacks are only three fifths of all other Persons." In 1857, in the *Dred Scott* decision, the U.S. Supreme Court declared blacks to be "a subordinate and inferior class of beings."[41] Following closely on this logic, within a year after the Dred Scott decision the Virginia Supreme Court ruled that "in the eyes of the law, so far certainly as civil rights and relations are concerned, the slave is not a person, but a thing."[42]

Women in Canada fared better but were denied the benefits of Personhood when, in 1876, a ruling in British common law declared that "Women are persons in matters of pains and penalties, but are not persons in matters of rights and privileges."

A few years later, in 1881, writing in *The American Law Review*, legal scholar George F. Canfield argued that "an Indian is not a person within the meaning of the Constitution . . . [Congress] may prevent an Indian from leaving his reservation, and while he is on a reservation it may deprive him of his liberty, his property, his life."[43]

In 1916 Emily Murphy was the first woman police magistrate in Alberta, Canada. In 1917 she successfully ran for the Senate, but Canadian Prime Minister Sir Robert Borden blocked her nomination on the basis that she was not considered a *person* under the British North America Act of 1867. She appealed to the Canadian Supreme Court, asking for clarification of a simple question: "Does the word 'persons' in Section 24, of The British North America Act, 1867, include female persons?" The Court's unequivocal response: NO!

In November 1935 Nazi Germany declared that Jews were "subjects" of the Reich but not "citizens" under the newly enacted Nuremberg Laws on Citizenship and Race. Article 4 (1) stated, "A Jew cannot be a citizen of the Reich. He cannot exercise the right to vote; he cannot hold public office." After the Nuremberg Laws of 1935, a number of additional Nazi decrees were issued that eventually outlawed the Jews completely, depriving them of their rights as human beings. Genocide was soon to follow.

In 1973, in the Roe v. Wade decision, Justice Harry Blackmun wrote that, "[If the] suggestion of Personhood [of the preborn] is established, the [abortion rights] case, of course, collapses, for the fetus' right to life is then guaranteed specifically by the [14th] Amendment."[44]

More recently, in May 2008, Cornell University created a "glow in the dark" human child by crossing human genes with a fluorescent gene from an Australian jellyfish. The embryo was destroyed before its third week of life. A spokesperson for the National Institutes of Health declared that "the Cornell work would not be classified as gene therapy in need of federal review, because a test-tube embryo (child) is not considered a *person* [emphasis mine] under the regulations."[45]

Personhood is the Path to Victory

Two maps: divine law and natural law; which strategies will the prolife movement follow in the 21st century? These maps draw from differing foundations of moral authority. On the one hand natural law has an unbroken history of failure, proving itself powerless to protect and respect human life and dignity. All too often it leads to human genocide and holocaust. Divine law, on the other hand, has the power to transform culture and government. It does this by first binding the consciences of individual men and women. God then raises these men and women to positions of power, influence and government. Romans 13:1-2 states that "there is no authority except from God, and those that exist have been instituted by God. Therefore whoever resists the authorities resists what God has appointed." Natural law relies on human reason to form a moral consensus, while divine law establishes moral absolutes that brook no compromise. One has an appearance of wisdom, the other the power of God.

Summary

It was not until Georgia Right to Life turned from following the map of natural law in the direction of God's Law that we begin to emerge from the wilderness of inaction, ineffectual law and lack of influence within the culture. From the very moment we made a decision at the Board level to follow God's ways we began experiencing a string of supernatural victories and advances that have resulted in many innocent lives being saved. Nothing has proven more pragmatic than taking a principled stand for life!

Chapter 3

Personhood: A Biblical Necessity

In short, . . . the best preparation for being a good politician, as well as a superior man in every other line, is to be a truly religious person.

William Wilberforce

But thanks be to God, who in Christ always leads us in triumphal procession, and through us spreads the fragrance of the knowledge of him everywhere. For we are the aroma of Christ to God among those who are being saved and among those who are perishing, to one a fragrance from death to death, to the other a fragrance from life to life.

2 Corinthians 2:14–16

I am a faith-based prolife activist, for which I make no apologies. Neither should the prolife movement. I am pro-Personhood BECAUSE. . . . God is pro-Personhood. The sanctity-of-life ethic is biblically revealed in over 50 passages of Scripture.[46] The prophets Isaiah and Jeremiah, as well as John the Baptist, were known by God in the womb, called by God, and in John's case even named by God and filled with the Holy Spirit "from his mother's womb" (Luke 1:15). The Bible reveals that the preborn have individuality, worth and purpose in the eyes of God. Personhood is the biblical teaching that establishes the foundation for all prolife activism. It is imperative that today's prolife community understand the importance of establishing our current prolife policy, strategy and political action on the same theological, philosophical and political basis that has enabled us to successfully promote human dignity throughout Western culture for the last two thousand years.

Biblical Doctrine of Imago Dei

Most of us are familiar with the classic hymn *Holy, Holy, Holy*, the refrain of which declares the eternal truth of "God in three Persons—blessed Trinity." One God in three distinct Persons—set apart from each other and yet equal—this is a great and profound mystery. Personhood exists within the Godhead.

When God created humankind He imparted the similar attribute of Personhood. Genesis 1:26–27 allows us to listen in on a conversation taking place within the Godhead: "Then God said, 'Let us make man in our image, after our likeness . . . .' So God created man in his own image, in the image of God he created him; male and female he created them."

In the original Hebrew this would have been translated

"Let us make man to be like us and to represent us." An example of this unity can be seen in the sacrament of marriage, where two "become one flesh" (Mark 10:8)—two persons, coequal in God's eyes and yet one in unity. This same unity is evidenced by an individual "person" being composed of the material (body) and the immaterial (soul and spirit). The Old Testament Hebrew words for "image" (*tselem*) and "likeness" (*demut*) both refer to something that is similar but not identical to the thing it represents. The attribute of "representation" separates all human life from the rest of God's creation.

This state of being "set apart," derived from the Hebrew word *qadosh*, is translated in our English Bibles as "holy." The New Testament Greek equivalent, *hagios*, fundamentally signifies "separated" and is translated into English as "sacred" or "sanctified."[47] From this concept we derive the term "sanctity of life." Theologian

Wayne Grudem observes, "While it is true that this difference with the rest of the animal kingdom is not absolute, it is also true that we are much more like God than all the rest of creation."[48] The concept that we are "separate"— and therefore "holy"—*because* we uniquely bear God's representation forms the foundation of human dignity and respect for all human life. Western civilization, its history and its law are based upon the Christian doctrine of "Imago Dei."

Imago Dei is Latin for the "image of God." To be created "Imago Dei" means being endowed with a body, soul and spirit (see 1 Thessalonians 5:23), a capacity to know and be known by God and a measure of autonomy and free will in the areas of thought and action that allow us to serve His purposes and glorify Him.

After the fall God's image in humanity was tragically distorted by sin, but it was *not* lost. This is explained by Grudem when he says (quoting Genesis 9:6), "Whoever sheds the blood of man, by man shall his blood be shed; for God made man in his own image." Even though men are sinful, there is still enough likeness to God remaining in them that to murder another person (to "shed blood" is an Old Testament expression for taking a human life) is to attack the part of creation that most resembles God, and it betrays an attempt or desire (if one were able) to attack God himself. Man is still in God's image. The New Testament gives confirmation to this when James 3:9 says that men generally, not just believers, "are made in the likeness of God."[49]

Perhaps the greatest argument for the sanctity of life is the incarnation itself. Christ Jesus took on human flesh and dwelt among us in order that he might redeem fallen humanity: "For God so loved the world, that he gave his only Son, that whoever believes in him should not perish but have eternal life. For God did not send his Son into the world to condemn the world, but in order that the world might be saved through him" (John 3:16–17). Accepting Jesus Christ by faith as our Lord and Savior begins the process of a progressive recovery of God's image. Paul says that as Christians we have a new nature that is "being renewed in knowledge after the image of its creator" (Colossians 3:10). At Christ's return there will be a complete restoration of God's image. "God has predestined us to be conformed to the image of his Son" (Romans 8:29; cf. 1 Corinthians 15:49), so that "when he appears we shall be like him" (1 John 3:2).

This is the biblical doctrine of *Imago Dei*. This teaching forms the foundation for the sanctity of human life throughout the Church Age.

The Historic Teaching of the Church

Western civilization's basic worldview on human dignity was formed in the 1st century by the Church and has been held firmly in Church teaching in every century since its inception. This truth has come to be known throughout the centuries as the *sanctity-of-life ethic* or the *culture of life*.

In every century of the Church Age the Holy Spirit has moved Church leadership to defend the image of God (*Imago Dei*) in humanity and, thereby, to oppose abortion and infanticide, as well as *planned barrenness*, while promoting compassion and mercy toward women in crisis pregnancy situations, the disabled, and the elderly infirm. Wherever the gospel of Jesus Christ was established, society was transformed from a pagan culture of death to a Christian culture of life in which human dignity was respected and human life protected.

Early Church Age (A.D. 95–A.D. 600)

Dr. George Grant, in his book *Third Time Around*, documents the history of the prolife movement through every century of Church history. He begins by quoting the *Didache* (a compilation of early apostolic teachings that we might define today as the first Christian bestseller). Written around A.D. 95, this work clearly states that "There are two ways the way of life and the way of death, and the difference between these two ways is great. Therefore, do not murder a child by abortion or kill a newborn infant."[50] Whenever the early Christians discovered an infant abandoned outside the city walls, they did everything they could to preserve its life and ensure its nurture. This was the hallmark practice of the early Christians in Rome; rescuing such infants from the wild animals that preyed upon unwanted foundlings became the basis for the establishment of our earliest Christian orphanages.[51] In the same manner, homes provided by Christians for temple prostitutes, cast out of their pagan temples when discovered to be pregnant, predated the homes for unwed mothers with which we are familiar. Nor is the modern Pregnancy Resource Center, with its emphasis on ministering to both mother and child, a new concept.

In A.D. 365 Basil of Caesarea, the pastor of a small congregation in Asia Minor, started just such a home to rescue women from a guild of local abortionists called "the sagae." He didn't stop there. He called upon his local lawmakers to outlaw the abortion guild he had discovered in his town. At the conclusion of a series of prolife messages to his local congregation, he called upon his fellow church members to boycott the sellers of women's cosmetics in his town. *Women's cosmetics?* you may ask. The gruesome truth Basil had uncovered is that the abortionists were harvesting human collagen from the babies they had aborted and selling it to cosmetologists in Egypt, who used it as a central ingredient in the manufacture of women's "beauty creams."[52]

Some things never change; currently a Swiss company, Neocutis, claims that skin cultured from fetal cells has many useful applications, including a line of cosmetics sold by the firm: "A small biopsy of fetal skin was donated following a one-time *medical termination* (emphasis mine), and a dedicated cell bank was established for developing new skin treatments. Originally established to promote wound healing and treat burns, this same cell bank today provides a lasting supply of cells for producing Neocutis's proprietary skin care ingredient: Processed Skin Cell Proteins (PSP'). The company assures the public that "No additional fetal biopsies will ever be required."[53] Former clinical instructor at Harvard Medical School Dr. Amy Tuteur asks the question, "Is there any moral difference between using the tissue of aborted fetuses to cure cancer and using it to cure wrinkles? And if it does matter, what does this tell us about the status of fetal tissue?"[54]

Basil was successful in driving the abortionists from his town. And throughout the entire Church Age we find the same success; whenever a pastor or group of pastors has taken a bold stand in condemnation of this practice within their community—the *culture of death* is banished.

The Church in the Middle Ages (A.D. 600–1400)

The Church in Medieval times faced the pagan practices of abortion, infanticide and the abandonment of deformed or unwanted children and eventually triumphed over each as the gospel of Jesus Christ permeated its culture. As an increasingly "Christianized" worldview came to hold sway in society, these ancient pagan practices fell into disrepute and for the most part ceased.

One of the most insidious practices to remain was that of abandoning children who were born with obvious disabilities. Yielding to despair and the stigma of bearing a "devil's child," even Christians participated in abandoning their children to the wild forces of nature.

At this time in history the Lord raised up a young Celtic princess by the name of Dympna Caelrhyn. Fleeing from her pagan father's incestuous advances, she settled in Gheel, a Flemish town near the city of Antwerp. After studying God's Word, she felt herself called to speak to the atrocities being committed against children and took a public stand against the killing of children with deformities and mental disabilities. Psalm 127:3 states categorically that "children are a heritage from the LORD, the fruit of the womb a reward." She reasoned that if the Bible teaches that these disabled children are "blessings" and that human life is "sacred," then that must mean that *all* human life is "special" in God's eyes and worthy of being protected and respected— no matter the degree of disability or dependency (mental impairment) or the manner of conception (illegitimacy). In addressing the special needs of children and adults in these circumstances, she stated: "All the starry hosts of heaven and of earth declare with one voice the glory bestowed on these sublime creatures of the Living God, these creatures made just a little lower than Himself. We can do no better than to acknowledge our acceptance of Him by our acceptance of them."[55] Her 8th-century children's home sheltered more than forty handicapped children, along with many mentally dependent adults.[56]

As fame of her actions spread, her pagan father, King Eadburh, arrived at her home and demanded that she return with him. When she refused, he murdered his daughter in a fit of rage. After her death the citizens of Gheel took over the ministry, and, amazingly, her project continues unabated to this day! "It includes a hospital for the mentally ill, a foundling center, an adoption agency, and the world's largest and most efficient boarding-out program for the afflicted and disturbed—run as a private and decentralized association by the Christian families of Gheel."[57]

While secular history portrays the time of the Middle Ages as "the Dark Ages," nothing could be further from the truth as it relates to the spiritual walk of average Christians and their understanding of the need to respect and protect all human life.

Prolife legislation in the 6th century was comprehensively and rigorously enforced. Emperor Justinian of Byzantium issued the following edict embodying Christian mercy and compassion in law:

> Those who expose children, possibly hoping they would die, and those who use the potions of the abortionist,

are subject to the full penalty of the law—both civil and ecclesiastical—for murder. Should exposure occur, the finder of the child is to see that he is baptized and that he is treated with Christian care and compassion. They may be then adopted . . . even as we ourselves have been adopted into the kingdom of grace. But, no one may claim as his own—under the rubric of lordship, legal obligation, or servile tenure—an exposed infant. Without distinction, those who are reared in this way by such persons are to be regarded as free and freeborn persons, and they may acquire and dispose of property as they wish, to their own heirs or others, untouched by any taint of servitude or legal subordination or condition of serfdom. This is to be enforced not only by the authorities of the provinces, but also by the bishops, by all officials, by civic leaders and officeholders, and by every government agency.[58]

For the first time in history the sanctity-of-life ethic was the prevailing worldview in all of Western civilization. Eastern Orthodox, Coptic, Celtic and Roman Catholic expressions of the Church all promoted the sanctity-of-life teaching. A short list of medieval prolife heroes includes Madedoc of Ferns (gave shelter to infants who survived primitive abortion surgeries at the hands of pagan Druids); Pastor John of Amathus (tore down the remnants of the old infanticide walls outside the city); Adamnan of Ions (in 697 he outlawed coercive abortion; Adamnan's law is still the basis of family policy in Ireland); Princess Bathild of Chelles (under her influence the French legal code was changed to reflect a prolife position, which remained intact for over a thousand years); Boniface of Crediton (prolife missionary and martyr to the Teutonic tribes of Germany); Good King Wenceslas of Bohemia (criminalized abortion); Queen Margaret of Scotland (unflinching intolerance of abandonment and abortion); Bonaventure of Bagnorea (waged war on merchants of abortifacients); Gregory the Great (d. 604); Cuthbert of Lindisfarne (d. 687); Giles Aegidius (d. 796); Clement Slovensky (d.916); Edburga of Winchester (d. 960); Dunstan of Canterbury (d. 988); Edward the Confessor (d. 1066); Sava of Trnova (d. 1235); Louis of France (d. 1270); and Elizabeth of Portugal (d. 1336).[59] Grant concludes, "By their faith and by their actions, these Christians brought about a revolution in human history. For the first time there was a consensus that life was sacred, that it ought to be protected, and that God would bless any culture that did."[60]

The Renaissance and the Enlightenment (A.D. 1400–1600)

The explosive development of science, technology, medicine and the arts transformed the culture of the Middle Ages. No institution was left untouched by this tsunami of knowledge known in secular circles as the Renaissance. The biblical underpinnings of the prevailing Christian culture were questioned by the new prophets of an ancient religion— secular pagan humanism. These prophets and evangelists of a resurgent religion transitioned to professors of learning in the churches and universities. Many of the new scholars questioned and then rejected the Christian worldview. "Nature abhors a vacuum," and the removal of biblical wisdom was replaced by a revival of pagan "wisdom."

The study of Greek and Roman philosophers dominated the courses of study at the universities and colleges of that day. Aristotle, Seneca, Cicero, Plato and Pythagoras were resurrected from the ashes of antiquity to displace Moses, David, Solomon and Paul. Jesus Christ, according to the prevailing thought, was a good man but certainly not the incarnate Creator God. This rejuvenated paganism impacted all levels of society, including the Church—doing much to neuter its message and subvert its gains.

The foundations for the sanctity of life that had been so carefully laid during the Middle Ages crumbled within a few decades, and the

Church, infected with pagan wisdom and a dependency upon human reason, lost its ability to restrain fallen humanity from reverting to its ancient practice of child sacrifice—with the result that the underlying view of the sanctity of life, at least for a time, collapsed.

By the middle of this age the impact of this return to a false set of values had led to the practice of wholesale destruction of innocent children. Gleaning from the scholarly work of Yale University professor John Boswell,[61] Grant asserts that as many as one in three children was aborted, abandoned or exposed in the countries of Spain, Italy and France. Among the poorer classes the rate crept as high as forty percent.[62] In Paris as many as thirty percent of all registered births ended in child abandonment, and in Florence, Italy, that figure rose to forty-five percent.[63] French philosopher and hero Jean-Jacques Rousseau, embodying the "enlightened" parenting style of his day, boasted that he had abandoned all five of his illegitimate children, placing each of them in an orphanage as soon as they were weaned.[64]

George Santayana proclaimed that "Those who cannot remember the past, are condemned to repeat it."[65] Influenced by the neo-paganism of our own time—currently in the United States it is estimated that forty percent of all women have abandoned a child in their womb to the abortionist's knife[66]— child and human sacrifice (including that of the elderly infirm, infants with disabilities, and embryos harvested for deadly human research) is unrestrained in Western culture.

The current prolife effort to limit surgical abortion via the strategy of incremental legal regulation is being rendered impotent by the increase of chemical abortion. A sexually libertine country like France is finding that its surgical abortion rate is falling.[67] Obviously this is not because France has placed incremental restrictions on access and availability of surgical abortions. No, the rate is falling due to the large increase in "self-administrated" abortion via easy access to chemical abortifacients.

This trend will continue as long as the women in a culture view the early stages of fetal development as simply a "blob of tissue." The only counter to this rising tide of death by "human pesticide" is to convince the prospective mother that she is carrying a "child" imbued with worth and dignity—a human being who should be protected by love and law. Personhood communicates this message. The current prolife strategy of allowing abortion in certain" justified" cases most definitely *does not*!

The Reformation and Counter Reformation (A.D. 1490–1630)

The tumultuous period of the Protestant and Catholic Reformations saw both branches of the Church engaged in condemning abortion in the strongest language:

> The unborn child . . . though enclosed in the womb of its mother, is already a human being . . . and should not be robbed of the life which it has not yet begun to enjoy. If it seems more horrible to kill a man in his own house than in a field, because a man's house is his place of most secure refuge, it ought surely to be deemed more atrocious to destroy an unborn child in the womb before it has come to light.
>
> John Calvin[68]

> Life is God's most precious gift. To scorn it by any sort of murderous act—such as the abortion of a child—is not merely an awful tyranny, it is a smear against the integrity of God as well. Suffer as we must, even die if need be, such rebellion against heaven must not be free to run its terrible courses.
>
> Ignatius Loyola[69]

Personhood: 19ᵗʰ Century

Upon her arrival in India, British missionary Anna Bowden attempted to rescue girls from the adherents of *Arya Samaj*, a cult of Hindu extremists who practiced *deyana*—female infanticide. She also raised her voice and used her influence as a Victorian debutante to lobby the British government to outlaw *sarti*—the ritual sacrifice of widows on the funeral biers of their husbands—and *kananda* cultic abortifacient procedures. At the time the British colonial policy of noninterference within the culture ruled the day, and her objections were ignored. After all, so the argument went, the ongoing trade with India had to be protected against disruption by a cultural reaction. The Hindu extremists appealed to Queen Victoria's viceroy and were pacified when Anna was commanded to remain silent.

But Anna could not be silenced; she insisted "that rescuing innocent human life was 'directly related' to her mission work and that, in fact, it was 'directly related to any form of Christian endeavor, humanitarian or evangelistic.'"[70] Anna's resolve puts many of our current prolife efforts to shame: "The mandate of Holy Writ is plain. We must clothe the naked, feed the hungry, shelter the shelterless, succor the infirm, and rescue the perishing. I can do no less and still be faithful to the high call of our Sovereign Lord."[71] Anna took seriously the biblical command to "rescue those who are being taken away to death" (Proverbs 24:11), forming a network of Christians providing an escape route for condemned widows and creating a group of prolife believers that disrupted the practices and procedures of the abortionists.

The Hindu response was immediate: Her adversaries burned down her mission complex, raped the young women who had been rescued from the abortionists and tortured and killed Anna. In the words of George Grant,

> Her daring example sparked a revival within the missionary community in India and her journals, published shortly

after her martyrdom, made a stunning impact throughout England. Perhaps most importantly of all, her commitment stimulated and mobilized the church to call on the government to fundamentally alter the essence of the policy of non-interference—not just in India, but wherever the gospel went out around the globe—and to enforce a universal legal code rooted in the Christian notion of the sanctity of life.[72]

Anna is only one of many examples of the men and women God raised up during the Victorian era to promote a sanctity-of-life ethic.

Personhood: 20th Century

"It is a poverty to decide that a child must die so that you may live as you wish." So said Mother Teresa of Calcutta. Born in 1910, Agnes Gonxha Bojaxhiu (Mother Teresa) came to be known by her 20th-century friends and followers as the "Saint of Calcutta." Her name became synonymous with Christlike charity and selfless service to the hungry, destitute and dying people she encountered on the streets of Kolkata (Calcutta), India.

Always an outspoken critic of abortion, in 1990 Mother Teresa took on the Supreme Court of the United States on the issue of Personhood. She had her attorneys file an *amicus curiae* (friend of the court) brief in the case of New Jersey v. Alexander Loce, et al.[73]

Alexander Loce was a young man who discovered that his fiancée was pregnant with his child. A day later he found out that she had scheduled an abortion at a Morristown, N.J. abortion mill. Upon entering the facility to attempt to persuade her not to kill their child, he was arrested for trespassing. The core issue in his case, which specifically addressed the issue of *when* Personhood attaches under the law, was whether the life of the unborn child is entitled to protection under the due-process clause of the fourteenth amendment. Mother Teresa filed this scathing rebuke:

America needs no words from me to see how your decision in Roe v. Wade has deformed a great nation. The so-called right to abortion has pitted mothers against their children and women against men. It has shown violence and discord at the heart of the most intimate human relationships. It has aggravated the derogation of the father's role in an increasingly fatherless society. It has portrayed the greatest of gifts—a child—as a competitor, an intrusion, and an inconvenience. It has nominally accorded mothers unfettered dominion over the independent lives of their physically dependent sons and daughters. And in granting this unconscionable power, it has exposed many women to unjust and selfish demands from their husbands or other sexual partners. Human rights are not a privilege conferred by government. They are every human being's entitlement by virtue of his humanity. The right to life does not depend, and must not be declared to be contingent, on the pleasure of anyone else, not even a parent or a sovereign.

The Constitutional Court of the Federal Republic of Germany recently ruled: "The unborn child is entitled to its right to life independently of its acceptance by its mother; this is an elementary and inalienable right which emanates from the dignity of the human being."

Americans may feel justly proud that Germany in 1993 was able to recognize the sanctity of human life. You must weep that your own government, at present, seems blind to this truth.[74]

Mother Teresa captured in a few words the sublime truth that the right to life is sacred (the "sanctity" issue) and inviolable, not granted by government and hence not to be abridged by any governing power or court.

Her comments directly confronted the Court with its legal positivism. Its finding in Roe v. Wade that the right to privacy, and hence abortion, was established for any woman seeking to end her pregnancy under a new "right to privacy" was based upon an "emanation" of the "penumbra" of the U.S. Constitution.

A 1965 ruling in the case of Griswold v. Connecticut,[75] involving a state's right to outlaw contraceptives, established for the first time the Constitutional "right of privacy" in a reproductive context. The Court justified its decision by declaring: "The foregoing cases suggest that specific guarantees in the Bill of Rights have penumbras, formed by emanations from those guarantees that help give them life and substance."[76] "Emanations" of "penumbras" constitute, at best, an ethereal foundation for the taking of an innocent human life and are directly at odds with the spirit of our founding fathers, who declared "that all men are endowed by their Creator with certain unalienable Rights, that among these are Life . . . ."[77] Mother Teresa rightly bases her argument on the "inalienable" right to life. An inalienable right is a right conferred by God, a right that cannot be abridged by government because it does not originate with the "lesser authority." The Church's teaching of the biblical doctrine of *Imago Dei* is the basis of our "inalienable right which emanates from the dignity of the human being."[78]

Personhood: In This Present Church Age

The revival of the study of pagan philosophers near the end of the Middles Ages ushered in an age of secular humanism, an age in which human wisdom and reason are elevated above faith, hope and love. The modern Church has in many ways acquiesced to this attack by elevating Aristotilian "wisdom" to the same status as godly wisdom. While it is true that all true wisdom originates from the character of God, it is also true historically that the acceptance and application of ancient pagan philosophy has led to syncretism and compromise within the Church and damaged the sanctity-of-life foundation in the culture.

Much of the modern prolife movement has also been infected with this pagan philosophy. Human, secular wisdom is promoted above Scriptural teaching and godly principle, and many of today's prolife apologists boast that there is no religious element to their defense of innocent human life.[79] They are in effect invoking a neo-pagan humanism as the basis for a right to life, not the explicitly Christian understanding that the right to life is inalienable, granted to every human being by God. By removing the distinctly biblical foundation they fall prey to espousing arguments of lesser power in an attempt to persuade a culture that is in desperate need of a set of "absolutes" to counter this relativistic approach to truth.

Today raw political pragmatism dictates prolife strategy. Prudence, as a moral character trait, has been redefined to allow for moral cowardice, inferior results and compromised standards, and biblical standards are cast as fanatic, idealistic and unachievable.[80] This is not surprising when the authorities cited by the leading prolife opponent to Personhood is based primarily on the philosophy of Aristotle.[81]

Catholic encyclicals, including *Humanae Vitae*, *Evangelium Vitae* and *Dignitatas Personae*, establish Personhood as a central teaching of the Roman Catholic Church. These "Instructions" call upon the Catholic faithful to uphold human dignity for the preborn, the disabled and the elderly infirm. An Instruction from the *Vatican Congregation for the Doctrine of the Faith* (CDF) on ethical issues dealing with biomedical research has this to say in its opening sentence: "The dignity of a person must be recognized in every human being from conception to natural death." *Dignitatas Personae* goes on to use the word "person" over 40 times. The central theme is the biblical teaching of *Imago Dei*.

Anglican author and theologian C. S. Lewis establishes this foundational premise in his prophetic work *The Abolition of Man* (1943), in which he warns that a world that refuses to question the ethical impact of its biomedical advances will eventually destroy human dignity and usher in a fearful new world . . . a world in which humankind is made in the image of Man and not in the image of God.

Dr. Francis Schaeffer and Dr. C. Everett Koop, with their release of a film series titled *Whatever Happened to the Human Race?* galvanized Protestants of all stripes and sent them forth in the early 1980's to do battle against abortion. For the first time in the 20th century Catholics, mainline Protestants and Evangelicals came together as co-belligerents to stand for the simple truth that abortion is wrong because God's Word says that we are endowed by our Creator with a basic right to life.

Summary

The gospel of Jesus Christ, bringing in its wake the Christian notion of the sanctity of life, has transformed Western culture repeatedly over the last two thousand years. The reality is that whenever the right to life message is separated from its spiritual and biblical foundation, it fails! Jesus warned us in Matthew 5:13, "You are the salt of the earth, but if salt has lost its taste, how shall its saltiness be restored? It is no longer good for anything except to be thrown out and trampled under people's feet."

The modern prolife movement has rejected the foundational truth of Scripture and replaced it with a neo-pagan humanist approach that has proven inadequate to confront the devaluing of human life through its most common expression, modern child sacrifice. When and only when the prolife movement of our day insists on returning to its biblical and historic roots can we expect the forces of evil to be put to flight by a revival of God's power working through His people. Personhood, as a movement, promotes the biblical teaching of *Imago Dei* and the spiritual disciplines of hopeful action coupled with faith-filled prayer that can expect to see the gates of Hell crumble as we march from prolife victory to prolife victory.

Chapter 4

Personhood: Principled Pragmatism

Policy, however, Sir, is not my principle, and I am not ashamed to say it. There is a principle above everything that is politic, and when I reflect on the command which says: "Thou shalt do no murder," believing its authority to be divine, how can I dare to set up any reasonings of my own against it?

William Wilberforce

Some Christians became skeptical of the importance of cardinal virtues because of their classical or pagan roots . . . They warily regarded it as too philosophical and not Scriptural enough. They preferred to talk about commandments and duties rather than about virtues.

Clarke Forsythe, AUL

For since, in the wisdom of God, the world did not know God through wisdom, it pleased God through the folly of what we preach to save those who believe. For Jews demand signs and Greeks seek wisdom, but we preach Christ crucified, a stumbling block to Jews and folly to Gentiles, but to those who are called, both Jews and Greeks, Christ the power of God and the wisdom of God.

1 Corinthians 1:21–25

Prolife Strategy Must Begin with Principle

Ten years ago the two most common charges brought against Georgia Right to Life for taking a strong biblical stand on life were (1) that what we were doing was political folly that would cause the movement harm and (2) that we were demonstrating a particularly insidious form of religious naiveté. The apostle Paul, writing to the Corinthian church, has this to say: "But God chose what is foolish in the world to shame the wise; God chose what is weak in the world to shame the strong" (1 Corinthians 1:27). Real, awe-inspiring power and wisdom are available from God through the gospel; Paul goes on in verse 28 to imply that this wisdom will be despised by those directed by classical Greek wisdom; see also verse 23, which speaks of God's wisdom even causing some religious people to stumble.

"Wait a minute," you may object. "Do we really need to discuss this religious part of Personhood? Can't you get straight to the point of why you think Personhood is a better prolife strategy than the current modus operandi?"

Many in the prolife movement make the fatal presumption that our doctrine is secondary to our strategy. You will often hear them piously declaring that anyone who injects theology into the equation is either on the religious fringe or "so heavenly minded that they are no earthly good." We in the Personhood movement are charged by these critics with being political novices, naïve when it comes to dealing with the governmental process. Terms like "fanatic", "absolutist," "moral perfectionist," and "principlist" are hurled in our direction as pejoratives, aimed at disparaging those who have founded their worldview on the Bible—God's Truth revealed to humanity.

These naysayers seek to establish a false dichotomy between principle and pragmatism, saying things like "You mustn't let your principle get in the way of a pragmatic outcome," as though implementing truth—"true Truth," as theologian Dr. Francis Schaeffer used to say—shouldn't be our *most pragmatic* objective. My personal favorite is "You Personhood people shouldn't hold so closely to principle because" (as they smugly observe) "the *best* is the enemy of the *good*." What I find so amusing is that this quote originated with the French humanist philosopher Voltaire, who also said, "I am very fond of truth, but not at all of martyrdom."

Might not this philosophy go a long way toward explaining why we, as a people, a movement, and a body politick, are so eager to accept "second best" rather than paying a price for achieving the highest possible expression of justice this world can afford? If that price is martyrdom, I can only respond, "Then, so be it." Few of us will ever be asked to pay that price, but the stark truth is that most of us are unwilling to even consider standing alone. We're embarrassed and incapacitated by the prediction that if we stand on principle we'll be marginalized as an organization, as individual politicians, or as a movement; we're unnerved by the bleak forecast that "the public and politicians will reject us!" Here is one instance where I actually agree with the pagan sage Cicero, who said that "Extremism in the defense of liberty is no vice. And moderation in the pursuit of justice is no virtue."

Haven't we been told for years that "the church has been built on the blood of the martyrs"? The truth, far too often, is that our own moral cowardice prevents us from achieving the policy objective of the prolife movement: respect for the Personhood of all human life, whether elderly, infirm, disabled, or preborn. We need to cease hurling pejoratives at each other and return to our root principle—to protect all innocent human life, from the earliest biological beginning until natural death. This means identifying the absolutes found in Holy Writ and establishing them as a beachhead of inviolable truth that must be acknowledged as natural law. For the prolife movement that line in the sand is the doctrine of *Imago Dei*.

My experience as PAC director of Georgia Right to Life, in combination with the empirical data we have seen over the course of these last ten years, has proven that the Personhood approach produces outstanding political and legislative gains, while accomplishing a dramatic shift in public opinion in the direction of a sanctity-of-life ethic. Simply put, over the last decade we have found that Personhood, with its emphasis on a biblical worldview, is the most pragmatic strategy a prolife organization can promote.

On July 20, 2010, Georgia became the first state in the nation to have many of its primary voters approve, via a nonbinding straw poll, a call for a Personhood amendment to its state constitution. In 46 counties Georgia voters said yes to the question "Do you support an amendment to the Georgia State Constitution so as to provide that the paramount right to life is vested in each human being from the moment of fertilization until a natural death?"[82] It passed overwhelmingly among Republican primary voters in *every* county with an average percentage of 75%. This fell to 72% in Democratic counties. Our largest and most liberal urban counties, surrounding metro Atlanta, approved the question 60% and 62% respectively.

A little over three months later—in the November 2010 elections—Georgia voters chose for the first time to elect candidates who were prolife without "exceptions" for *every* statewide constitutional office! Not only did they not endorse exceptions, but every office—from governor to lieutenant governor to attorney general, all the way down to public service commissioner (nine offices total)—declared their support for a Personhood amendment to Georgia's constitution. These remarkable political victories didn't occur in a vacuum but were the result of a decade of a focus on Personhood educationally, politically, and legislatively.

Personhood is the only prolife strategy that will win in the 21st century because it is the only strategy in which the wisdom and power of Almighty God can be manifest in such a manner "that no human being might boast in the presence of God" (1 Corinthians 1:29). Our prolife worldview needs to change.

Legal and Political Implications of a Biblical Worldview

What do we mean by a worldview? A worldview may be defined as "the general understanding a community possesses about the world in which it exists."[83] When the Bible informs how we interpret the reality around us, we call this a biblical worldview. All Christians are in fact commanded to practice such a worldview. The apostle Paul instructed the members of the church at Philippi to "Have this mind in you, which was also in Christ Jesus . . ."

Our nation's founding charter, the Declaration of Independence, states that "we have been endowed by our Creator with certain unalienable rights" and that "among these are life, liberty and the pursuit of happiness." The term "unalienable" is archaic, but it is synonymous with the somewhat more familiar "inalienable." In the prolife context this means that government does not confer our right to life; instead, it comes from God and cannot be abridged by government, unless that right is granted by God as a legitimate exercise in times of war or other occasions.[84] As we have seen in our earlier discussion of *Imago Dei*, the Personhood of the preborn is a biblical concept originating with God. Personhood, therefore, must also be classified as an inalienable right conferred by God and not by government.

Several purist factions within the Right to Life movement refuse to endorse the objective of Personhood because they claim that we are in effect petitioning government to define and authorize Personhood. This is simply not true! Personhood already exists, in exactly the same manner that the right to life exists—as an inalienable right granted by God. Civil government cannot grant this right because it doesn't originate with civil government. Personhood can and must be recognized by government as a superior right. In fact, a government that refuses to acknowledge God as the originator of both of these basic rights runs the risk of incurring His judgment. The purists fear that if a Personhood challenge would somehow actually make it to the U.S. Supreme Court we would lose the battle and the war would be over; the government, they fear, would redefine Personhood as something less than its biblical reality.

But didn't an act of judicial fiat already usurp our God-given right to life in 1973? The U.S. Supreme Court ruled that preborn children do not have this inalienable right, granted by their Creator. Has this unbiblical and unconstitutional ruling quashed our courage to petition our government for correction of that egregious assault on human dignity? No! Year after year we march on our respective capitols and support laws that challenge this flawed ruling. We will never stop until our courts or legislatures have reversed or nullified this misguided ruling.

We do not fear a negative ruling from the U.S. Supreme Court. Historically, a bad ruling has in fact served as the very catalyst for change in public policy. Dred Scott v. Sandford, 1858, ruled that a black person could not be a citizen under our law. "[T]he tiered Personhood that Dred Scott allowed suggests that rights ostensibly owed to all people by virtue of their Personhood are not owed to certain groups of people."[85] This adverse ruling did much to fuel to the abolitionist movement; our country engaged in civil war before the law recognized the full Personhood of Blacks. In point of fact, the ruling per se was *never* reversed. By the same token, we shouldn't wait on an overturning of Roe v. Wade before engaging in public dialogue. The need for Personhood policy is *now*, regardless of Roe's final disposition! Ours is a 21st century human rights movement and must not be summarized by a single legal objective!

Our primary objective as a prolife movement has been the reversal of Roe v. Wade. Perhaps the prolife movement is ill served in continuing this pursuit, *if* this course of action means abandoning Personhood on the basis that it may—*may*—result in an adverse ruling, somehow establishing a right to abortion or incorporating a flawed definition of Personhood into U.S. law.

James Bopp Jr., legal counsel for National Right to Life, has often cautioned that the loss of a Supreme Court case centered around Personhood is not costless. He is probably correct, but the fear of loss has resulted in the prolife movement abandoning its quest for Personhood in favor of placing as many limits on abortion as are prudently possible. This strategy has been nominally successful over the years. Studies have claimed that by "fencing in abortion" through such means as a twenty-four-hour waiting period, parental consent laws, and laws that endorse abortion for certain classes of humans (those conceived as the result of rape or incest), the incidence of abortion has decreased.

But many more studies have shown that the real reason surgical abortions have decreased is the rapid proliferation of chemical abortion. The problem is that this form of legal positivism does nothing to address the root problem. The root problem? Too many women see the child in their womb as nothing more than a blob of reproductive tissue. By focusing our efforts on placing incremental limits on abortion, we allow women to continue to argue for their personal right to privacy while depersonalizing their unborn children. Instead we should be focusing on the fact that they are terminating the life of a young child, one who has rights and who is owed responsibilities under our laws.

Summary

Personhood is the only strategy that takes us beyond the abortion rights debate and appeals to the conscience of an abortion-minded mother to spare her unborn child.[86] Personhood as a strategy transfers the focus from women's health and rights, transforming the argument into a human rights issue that transcends abortion and allows us to address the entire spectrum of sanctity-of-life issues, including cloning, IVF, euthanasia, and the newly emerging eugenics movement.

Unfortunately, the current interpretation of our United States Constitution limits its protection to "born" persons. Whether this was intentional or a result of simple ignorance of prenatal science in the 18th century, it is clear that this limitation implicitly violates the doctrine of *Imago Dei* and that it has resulted in a branch of the prolife movement that is focusing its educational and legislative efforts on promoting Personhood as the answer to the emerging biotech issues facing us in the 21st century.

Chapter 5

Personhood:
Future of the Prolife Movement

[W]e move from the *taking* of life [abortion] through *making* life [IVF] to what I have somewhat crudely termed the *faking* of life: the capacity of developments in the fields of nanotechnology and cybernetics to manipulate, enhance and finally perhaps supplant biological human nature.[87]

Chuck Colson and Nigel Cameron

And the LORD said, "Behold, they are one people, and they have all one language, and this is only the beginning of what they will do [Tower of Babel]. And nothing that they propose to do will now be impossible for them."

Genesis 11:6

Simply put, Personhood is nothing less than the prolife battleground of the 21st century. As we have shown historically and doctrinally, Personhood is the biblical teaching of the sanctity of life. Throughout Church history, the doctrinal teaching on this issue has been based on Genesis 1: 26-27: humankind is created "in the image of God" (Imago Dei) and therefore, has worth at all stages of life. This is the bedrock of Western civilization's understanding and practice of human dignity. We are also told in the Gospels that John the Baptist was known by God, called by God, named by God, and then filled by God with the Holy Spirit while still in his mother's womb. John the Baptist is an example of the biblical worldview of Personhood.

Let's contrast our biblical perspective with an emerging secular worldview. The following excerpt was taken directly from the FAQs listed on the website of Peter Singer, the DeCamp professor of bioethics at Princeton University:[88]

> **Q.** You have been quoted as saying: "Killing a defective infant is not morally equivalent to killing a person. Sometimes it is not wrong at all." Is that quote accurate?
>
> **A.** It is accurate, but can be misleading if read without an understanding of what I mean by the term "person."[89]

Singer argues his case in his book *Unsanctifying Human Life.* While he does believe that the "right to life" should be granted to all "persons" equally, his definition of "person" is extremely narrow, excluding not only preborn and disabled children and the elderly infirm, but also pefectly formed born infants through 18 months of age. Singer goes on to declare that his own mother would probably no longer be alive if he were the sole caregiver in his family.[90]

One would expect to hear that Singer's position is on the loopy fringe of public policy discussions. Surprisingly, his prestigious position at Princeton and his vast international influence have earned him acclaim as one of the leading bioethicists of our day. Don't be surprised if twenty years from now we find his positions on "Personhood" to be encased in law, applied by our hospitals' ethics boards, and resulting in the entombment and execution of embryonic children at our research laboratories and universities.

The Right to Life movement is "fifteen years behind the curve in addressing and responding to this threat,"[91] cautions prolife bioethicist Wesley Smith. Our narrow anti-abortion focus in the 20th century failed to equip prolife citizens to counter a host of

21st century issues. Even though national prolife groups continue to warn of these emerging threats to human dignity, the local grassroots supporter is not engaged. We need to adjust our strategy and message to one of Personhood so that we can successfully transition our base from being primarily anti-abortion to recognizing and protecting the sanctity of life wherever it is being assaulted.

It's No Longer Just about Abortion

An example of the failure of the Right to Life movement is its lack of response to a new and emerging challenge against the sanctity of all life, as seen in the state of Missouri in 2006. On November 6 of that year Missourians approved a "ban on cloning." Unfortunately, it was a fake ban that actually allowed cloning for "therapeutic" purposes. Put off by the use of the word "therapeutic," the grassroots prolife voter failed to discern that a human life hung in the balance. The ban changed the Missouri constitution to allow for a human child, brought into existence in a laboratory through somatic cell nuclear transfer (SCNT), to be "grown" for 14 days, subjected to human experimentation, and then destroyed. The prolife base failed to understand the issue, recognize the danger, or reject this assault on human life and dignity. More dramatically, this case verified that the word "therapeutic," when placed in front of any unethical or life-assaulting biomedical practice, assures that the vast majority of voters will condone the practice in question—in this case the destruction of children at an embryonic level. After all, so the thinking goes, the procedure *must* be moral if it seeks to discover cures for "grandma's" Alzheimer's or Michael J. Fox's Parkinson's disease or if it embodies the promise that someone like Christopher Reeve will walk again.

Destruction of human children at the embryonic level has now expanded beyond research laboratories to be enshrined as a "procreative right" of infertile couples seeking to become parents. It is not uncommon to create between 15 and 20 embryonic children at one time and then, through the process of selective reduction or the eugenic practice of pre-implantation genetic diagnosis (PGD), to kill all but one or two of those children. As tragic as it may be for a couple to struggle with infertility, when did it become acceptable for a couple's "right to parent" to supersede another's "right to life"? Infertility is not a justification for murder. Neither is infertility untreatable. A prolife couple must be fully informed of all options before embarking on a path that assures the IVF clinics and biotech industry more human subjects to sacrifice on the altar of technology.

Drug companies and biotech businesses need human subjects in order to perfect their products; steady supplies of human embryos are needed in order to conduct these lethal experiments. Because fertility clinics cannot possibly supply the large number of embryos needed, the biotech industry has resorted to a transgenic solution: combining 98% human DNA with 2% cow DNA to form a human-animal hybrid known as a "chimera." As mentioned earlier, Cornell University in May of 2008 created a "glow in the dark" human child by crossing human genes with a fluorescent gene from an Australian jellyfish. The embryo was destroyed before its third week of life, and a spokesperson for the National Institutes of Health explained that "the Cornell work would not be classified as gene therapy in need of federal review, because a test-tube embryo [child] is not considered a person under the regulations."[92]

Our efforts to promote a culture of life in the 21st century require that we develop a clear and consistent message to alert our culture to the dangers that lie ahead if the definition of "person" is allowed to be eroded from its historical meaning. Personhood is the clear battleground of the prolife movement in our century.[93]

Personhood: Today's Debate . . . Tomorrow's Future

Our nation is unique in that it was founded upon the Judeo-Christian belief that every human being "was endowed by their

Creator with certain unalienable rights" and that "among these are life, liberty and the pursuit of happiness." The right to life is a person's most basic right. Without its protection all other rights become moot.

Seldom will you find disagreement with this premise; the arguments arise when we as a nation attempt to answer the questions of "when" our rights attach and "who" qualifies as a person under the law. Dred Scott v. Sandford answered these questions in one way—and Nazi Germany in another. In the United States our U.S. Supreme Court wrongly limits the right to life to "born persons."

Over the past 37 years the debate over this complex question has usually centered around traditional prolife issues, more particularly abortion. But with the emergence of new biotechnologies, the debate must widen from the ethics of life and death to the ethics of human nature and what it means to be created in "the image of God." This is another question altogether: the *why* of human dignity and the right to life. It is this question that serves as the foundation for a prolife ethic. The prolife movement must mature beyond the singular goal of "saving babies" and engage our current "culture of death" with a return to the foundational premise that each and every innocent human being must be respected and protected—from its earliest biological beginning until its natural death. Personhood is the means.

The Making, Taking, and Faking of Human Life

The century of the 1800's has come to be known as the Industrial Age, while the 20th century has been dubbed the Nuclear Age. The 21st century, in contrast, seems destined to be remembered as the Biotech Age. Modern secularist prophet Ray Kurtzwiel has proven empirically that there is an exponential curve in our current growth of biomedical knowledge. His sage prediction is that the amount of biomedical knowledge acquired since the dawn of history will double within the next decade, and he goes on to make the unbelievable assertion that it will double *again* in the following decade.[94]

Professor Michael Sleasman, managing director and research scholar for The Center for Bioethics & Human Dignity, explains that, "while many of the ethical questions of the late 20th Century dealt with bio-ethical concerns over the beginning and end of life issues (the making, and taking of human life), the questions raised by these new, these emerging technologies threaten to change the nature of the human species and the very essence of what it means to be human."[95]

"Germ-line intervention" is a term that describes the ability of our current state of bio-science to alter the human genome in ways that will be transmissible through normal sexual reproduction. This new technology has to do with the use of genetically altered eggs or sperm to correct or improve the genetic makeup of a resulting child. On its surface this technology promises a generational cure for diseases like Tay-Sachs, which afflicts Eastern European Jews, and Sickle Cell Anemia, afflicting primarily the Black race. This is a needed objective. The problem is that once a genetic change is made to the human genome and is allowed to propagate within the human gene pool, it cannot be undone. Put in another way, once the genie is out of the bottle there is no way of putting it back in. This raises the sinister specter of irreversible harm. From selling the "therapeutic" objective of germ-line intervention to our culture it would be only a short logical hop before we would be presented with the darker side of human enhancement known as eugenics.

A culture that rejects the absolute truth that God created humanity in his own image will naturally evolve to demand that humans create humans in the image of man. Transhuman enhancement, designer babies, cyborgs (human-machine cybrids), and chimeras (human-animal hybrids) suddenly come into focus as desirable objectives. The advancement of the human species by human means is in fact the goal of a new philosophy that is being presented in our nation's colleges and universities. No longer, so the trans-human philosophers enthuse, will we be called *Homo sapiens*—humankind will now be designated *Homo perfectus!* In contrast, Personhood as a public policy not only protects preborn children, but as the basic embodiment of Imago Dei, assures the protection of what it means to be human by establishing a benchmark for human dignity.

Western civilization is at a critical juncture. According to U.S. Congressman Brad Sherman, a member of the United States House Science Committee, the unprecedented capabilities of emerging biotechnologies have set the stage for a technological revolution which he has referenced as analogous only to the development of nuclear technology. That our culture has indeed reached an ethical crossroads is evidenced by the following statements made by American congressmen at a "nano-policy roundtable" held in 2006: "Now, like my colleagues, I do not have any answers. Rather, I hope to identify some of the questions. I know that the right time to start thinking about these questions is now. . . . What is the definition of a human?" (U.S. Congressman Brad Sherman).[96] And "We are talking about a suite of technologies that are going to revolutionize the way we do things and how we live. And the questions are 'How will that happen?' and 'What will we do as this unfolds?' (Marty Spritzer, speaking on behalf of Representative Sherwood Boehlert, chairman of the House Science Committee).[97]

What are the policy implications of the emerging medical technologies? The courts are demanding both definitions and laws. Christian bioethicist, Nigel Cameron, the president and cofounder of the Institute on Biotechnology & the Human Future, has stated, "The problem is brought into ready focus by the manner in which bioethics has essentially emerged as the conjoined twin of bio-policy." He goes on to predict that two terms will dominate public policy in the 21st century—transhumanism and eugenics.

Who lives and who dies? Who benefits from our finite medical resources? Whose lives may be sacrificed in order that others may live? If only "persons" benefit, who qualifies as a "person"? The questions have been posed, but their answers require a deeper look into the nature of ethics, policy, ideas, and actions.

In the 20th century it was sufficient for Right to Life advocates to focus on being anti-abortion. But this single focus will *not* be sufficient in light of the new "killing fields" of the 21st century. Our role in advocating Personhood is to facilitate, educate, and disseminate a biblical worldview within the Church, leading to a response within the larger grassroots prolife movement, one that will place our policy and strategy soundly on the biblical foundation of the whole range of issues embodied in the phrase "sanctity of life," one that will stand the tests of time and fickle public opinion and defend human dignity beyond our present age. It is no longer just about abortion.

Summary

Because we bear the image of God, all humankind—by extension *every* human life—possesses a "special-ness," a unique value and worth that demands respect and legal protection. Each human life, from its earliest stage of development, is a unique Person who bears God's likeness and deserves the same protection under law that is afforded all other "persons" in our society. For this reason all human life must be respected and protected *in law*.

This respect is due regardless of the manner of conception, whether through the marital act or through a heinous act of rape or incest; whether the egg is fertilized "in vitro" (IVF) or through the "ex utero" process of somatic cell nuclear transfer (SCNT), otherwise know as cloning. Regardless of the manner, age, or degree of disability or dependency, a human life has immeasurable worth in the eyes of God—an inestimable, intrinsic value that must be acknowledged by the culture and protected in its code of law.

Chapter 6

Personhood: Prudential, Political, and Legal Objections

A wise leader advocates his cause in a judicious and prudent manner; he is neither radical nor reactionary.

William Wilberforce

People of faith, it seems, are particularly susceptible to imprudence when it comes to their involvement in political and social causes.

Clarke Forsythe

Losing is not costless.

James Bopp, Jr.

The Problem with Prudence

Biblical prudence is Scripture wisely applied to real life situations. Beginning with the biblical revelation of God's character and ways, we seek to apply our knowledge of Him to the problems we face in life.

The Bible says that a prudent man foresees danger and hides himself from it (see Proverbs 22:3). Indeed, the writer of Proverbs has much to say about prudent people; Prudence helps a man discern his way (14:8); the prudent gives thought to his steps (verse 15); the prudent is crowned with knowledge (verse 18); the prudent ignores an insult (12:16); and whoever heeds reproof is prudent (5:5). Clarke

Forsythe, former president of Americans United for Life, has noted that "Prudence is essential in all that we do *because it makes zeal effective.*"[98] As Forsythe points out, prudence tops the list of Aristotle's Four Virtues. Who could be against prudence?

Orthodoxy v. Orthopraxy

Today's prolife debate does not center around the definition of the godly character quality of prudence; rather, the debate rages around the manner it is to be applied in the context of our postmodern world. This is not a question of orthodoxy (right opinion) as much as it is a debate over orthopraxy (correctness of action or practice).

The apostle Paul has much to say about competing in long-distance running. In his first letter to the Corinthian church he challenges, "Do you not know that those who run in a race all run, but only one receives the prize? Run in such a way that you may win" (1 Corinthians 9:24 NASB). Paul goes on, "Therefore I run in such a way, as not without aim . . ."(verse 26). The "aim" of the prolife movement is, and has always been, a human life amendment recognizing the inalienable right to life for all innocent human life. Personhood, as defined under divine law, is the objective.

Sadly, the current prolife movement gives lip service to this objective. They "prudently" opposes those who make it the focus of their strategy. By coining the term "moral perfectionism" to define those of us who hold to a principled objective, the critics within the movement convince others that our position is somehow opposed to incremental gains as we quest to win the prize. Nothing could be further from the truth. We all support incremental gains as we race toward the finish line. By advocating a state Personhood amendment rather than demanding a federal Personhood amendment, we demonstrate our understanding of an "all-or-something" approach. Prudence, we believe, demands that we first achieve a consensus in 33 different state legislatures that Personhood is the desired objective and then move on to press for the ratification of a Personhood amendment to our U.S. Constitution.

The problem is that we, as a movement, have separated this incrementalism from our moral purpose—and by so doing are damaging our own objective and delaying justice. Incrementalism is not the problem—a flawed version of incremental orthopraxy—is!

Wilberforce Repents of Flawed Incrementalism

There is within the movement a prevailing opinion that a biblically sound objective is unattainable in a fallen world. This has led to the practice of erecting legal fences around the social evil of child killing, in the hope that regulation will eventually lead to prohibition—when we should in fact be "running with endurance" toward the prize at hand: the legal emancipation of the preborn. By accepting regulation as our primary strategy, we in effect weaken our argument that emancipation is our objective.

Nowhere in history do we find a better example of the struggle between misguided incrementalism and principled prudential pragmatism than in the worldwide struggle to emancipate slaves. It is informative that the renowned English abolitionist William Wilberforce initially succumbed to this same flawed reasoning; he worked for nearly two decades to merely regulate the slave trade in the hope that with more restrictions on the slave owners the slaves' living conditions would be improved. In the early days of the Abolition Society it was hotly debated whether it would be more effective to strive for full emancipation of the slaves (declaring them to be Persons under law) or to settle for the lesser goal of banning the slave trade and then working toward emancipation. At the time, "Wilberforce argued that, of the two, abolition would be easier to achieve, and in the process, the public would be educated on the evils of slavery."[99]

This reasoning was prudent in some respects and foolish in

others. It was sensible to engage in a plan to shape public opinion about the evils of slavery as a necessary step toward the emancipation of the slaves, but it was foolish to expect that the evils of slavery would be averted simply by outlawing the abuses. The modern-day equivalent would be focusing all of our efforts on the overturning of Roe, as opposed to pressing for recognition of the Personhood of all human beings.

After twenty years of abolitionist effort, the Slave Trade Act was passed in 1807. The act may have abolished the slave trade in the British Empire, but it did nothing to eradicate slavery per se. Tragically, the practice remained legal for another two and a half decades. The immediate effect was that in order to avoid having their ships confiscated, British captains simply threw their captive slaves overboard. This flawed example of incrementalism highlights the tragic results possible from expecting that good can be effected simply by fencing in evil; in this case the strategy was justified on the basis of the need to raise public awareness.

We see the same lame argument being promoted in defense of the Partial Birth Abortion Ban Act. Some prolife leaders have admitted that this ban, while not saving lives, would at least keep the issue in the news. In fact, the language Supreme Court Justice Anthony Kennedy uses in describing—in very graphic detail—precisely how an abortionist can circumvent the law by impaling the child legally, will horrify anyone willing to take the time to actually read the ruling.[100]

Personhood activists agree with the need to raise public awareness as an incremental, prudential step toward our ultimate objective, but they vehemently disagree with the premise that "we must do evil that good may come." Our experience in Georgia has shown that by focusing public debate on the issue of the Personhood of the preborn we are in fact laying the foundation for protecting the Personhood of the elderly infirm, the severely disabled, and those discriminated against on a "eugenic" basis, such as children with Down Syndrome.[101] There is no essential disagreement that our application of prudence demands incremental gains; public opinion is undeniably central to upholding justice over the longer term. We simply allege that Personhood is a more prudential argument than is partial-birth child killing when promoting our issues in the public square.[102]

According to Wilberforce's biographer David J. Vaughan, Wilberforce realized his error:

> [H]e hoped that once the trade was abolished the slave owners would of necessity improve their treatment of their slaves. Without a fresh supply of new slaves, they would take better care of the health and lives of the existing ones. As the slaves' lot improved through education, both spiritual and intellectual, they would be encouraged to marry and develop a stable family life. Over time it was hoped that they would become a free peasantry.
>
> This "amelioration" argument, as it was called, turned out to be fallacious, for it assumed that the slave owners would act in a rational manner; that is, in a way that was really in their best interests. But evil is not rational. Once the trade was abolished the owners' treatment of the slaves remained as brutal as before.[103]

The attempts to regulate slavery resulted simply in the slave owners coming up with new and less humane ways to circumvent the law. (Sound familiar? It is well established that abortionists have devised imaginative ways to circumvent many of our prolife regulatory requirements.) This led to an increase in the misery of the slaves, along with an acceptance by the citizenry that everything that could possibly be done under law to alleviate the slaves' suffering was being done. The tragic result: a prolonging of the slaves' suffering and delayed emancipation.

Another popular biographer, Eric Metaxas, author of the book *Amazing Grace*, on which a recent movie highlighting Wilberforce's life is based, wrote of Wilberforce's own epiphany regarding the matter:

> It was in 1818, after many failed attempts to pass the Slave Registry Bill, that Wilberforce and Clapham began at last to think of emancipation as the only solution to the sufferings of the West Indies slaves. The horrors that Wilberforce and his Clapham colleagues now discovered, eleven years after the abolition of the trade, shocked them. All hopes that the slaves' situation might have been slowly improving were dashed. . . . So once again the course was clear: immediate emancipation by political means.[104]

Wilberforce repented of his failed attempts to regulate the slave trade into submission. His political friends advised him that this course would not be prudent under the current political climate in Parliament, due to the severe recession in which the country was embroiled and the domestic unrest it had bred. This did not deter Wilberforce. In fact, it was from this point in time that the battle to emancipate the slaves began to turn in the abolitionists' favor. I believe that we as a movement need to repent in a similar manner.

What Prudence Is Not

Highly esteemed Notre Dame Law School professor emeritus Charles Rice has this to say: "I understand that certain prolife organizations oppose the petition drive to place this proposal [personhood amendment] on the Michigan ballot. That opposition, in my opinion, is irresponsible. The proposal is prudent, timely, and positive."[105] As a former law professor, he claims that the Personhood effort in Michigan satisfied the conditions necessary for prudence. The lesson: Personhood opponents must apply prudence differently.

It is always prudent to plan for victory, yet many in the prolife movement actually aim for much less. They do this by specifically lowering the standards by which they define success. Unfortunately and all too often what the opponents of Personhood demand is a deeply flawed expression of prudence that actually resembles moral cowardice and an unwillingness to stand alone rather than aiming at a godly standard and expecting to succeed. This has been demonstrated time and time again by those who set low expectations, both politically and legislatively.

It has been said that if you aim at nothing you're sure to hit it! In truth, these prolife advocates do hit their targeted objectives more often than not. The real loss is that these victories often come at the price of a higher good that could have been accomplished had they demonstrated more prudence and less timidity. Tragically, it gets worse: The real catastrophe is when these misguided leaders undermine a well-reasoned plan to effect long-lasting prolife gains, either politically or legislatively, and justify their actions as prudence. They destroy by their "pagan piety" the very objectives for which they claim to be fighting; they destroy the very notion of Personhood.

Examples of this abound, the most recent of which have taken place in South Dakota, Colorado, Georgia, and Montana. In each case a serious, well-planned, and well-executed campaign was led by a new generation of prolife leadership with the goal of shifting public opinion toward a principled prolife position. All involved the issue of Personhood. In every case a faction of the prolife leadership denounced the effort as imprudent. What is confusing is that both sides were claiming to be operating under this preeminent (cardinal) virtue.

In my opinion, Clarke Forsythe, senior counsel for Americans United for Life, has taken a more oppositional stance against the Personhood strategy than any other prolife leader. Yet he states that,

"It's useful that Georgia and other states are debating a human life amendment at the same time that Professors Robert

George and Christopher Tollefson have released *Embryo: A Defense of Human Life*. . . . If public debate about the status of a human embryo is inevitable and necessary (as their book recognizes), then debate about whether a state constitutional amendment is an *effective means* [italics original] to the embryonic human is also inevitable and necessary."[106]

In Georgia the debate has been highly effectual! We introduced the amendment in 2007, and by 2010 most of Georgia's legislators had publicly stated their support. This actually became a wedge issue in the gubernatorial debates during the 2010 primary, and the candidate who defended Personhood is now the governor of Georgia.

Political Objections

In many ways this is one of the simplest objections to deal with. Our opponents say that Personhood cannot win and that it does not work! But Georgia has ten years of empirical political data to categorically demolish this lie (see Appendix 2). In point of fact it wasn't until we began pursuing a principled objective in politics that we began to see the amazing results that defied conventional political "wisdom" and silenced our critics within the prolife movement. Clarke Forsythe says, "It is not enough to simply rhetorically defend a principle; the challenge in a world of constraints is effectively achieving the greatest good possible." I could not agree more! In Georgia we have done both.

Within six months of adopting a "no rape and incest" criterion for political endorsement, every Executive Committee officer serving the Georgia Republican Party was on board with a "no exceptions" position on abortion. After ten years of holding the line on this policy, nine statewide constitutional offices are held by an elected official who publicly defends the fact that life is sacred, that it begins at conception, and that there are no acceptable exceptions for abortion other than the rare situation in which the mother's life is indeed endangered by a continuation of the pregnancy. These public servants believe that sound medical practice even in this situation would dictate that every effort be made to save both lives.

Legal Objections

This is perhaps the most effective objection to Personhood, not because the legal arguments are persuasive but because most of us rely on the "experts" to inform us regarding legal matters, particularly when the issues deal with the stratospheric heights of U.S. Constitutional law. If these legal advisers say we are to "fear" the outcome of a set of actions, we believe we had better heed their sage warning. That would indeed be the prudent direction if every one of the prolife attorneys agreed, but they do not; they are in fact deeply divided on the issue.

Thomas More Law Center, Liberty Counsel, David Gibbs Law Firm (Terri Shaivo's attorney), Family Research Council, and American Center for Law and Justice are just a sampling of the organizations that are breaking ranks with the conventional legal wisdom of the past and have stepped forward to provide counsel to our Georgia legislators on Personhood.

Personhood has always been the policy objective of the modern prolife movement. There is no disagreement on this point from any faction of prolife leadership. Dr. John (Jack) Willke, former president of National Right to Life, articulates the "Ultimate Prolife Goals" in his 1985 book *Abortion: Questions &* Answers:[107]

"The ultimate prolife goal is quite direct and very simple. Prolifers want an amendment to the U.S. Constitution, to the Canadian Charter of Rights that will give equal protection under the law, to all living humans from the time their biologic life begins at fertilization until natural death. Understanding that such a goal remains yet in the future, prolife people have an intermediate goal. It is a Constitutional Amendment returning the right to make decisions about abortion to each individual state."[108]

In 1981 Dr. Willke, as acting president for National Right to Life, commissioned a young attorney by the name of James Bopp Jr. to construct a human life amendment (HLA). Working under a grant from the National Right to Life Educational Trust Fund,[109] Mr. Bopp crafted what later became known as the National Right to Life Committee (NRLC) Amendment. Another, competing amendment was known as the Garn Amendment. Bopp himself observes "that the NRLC Amendment [drafted in 1981] meets all of the goals of the right-to-life movement and would provide the fullest legal protection to the unborn."[110]

In March of 2007 Georgia Right to Life sponsored a bill in the Georgia House (H.R. 536) that was based on the language of the NRLC Amendment. The amendment was modified because we were not legislating at a federal level, attempting instead to pass the nation's first paramount human life amendment at a state level. This was an objective Dr. Willke identified as needful if we as a movement were unable to pass such an amendment at a federal level.

In the summer of 2007 James Bopp Jr., then legal counsel for National Right to Life, Focus on the Family, and Family Research Council, published a paper that attacked the effort.[111] The essence of his argument centered on four objections:

> The Supreme Court's current makeup assures that a declared federal constitutional right to abortion remains secure for the present. This means that now is not the time to pass *state* constitutional amendments or bills banning abortion because:
> (1) such provisions will be quickly struck down by a federal district court,
> (2) that decision will be affirmed by an appellate court,
> (3) the Supreme Court will not grant review of the decision,

and

(4) the proabortion attorneys who brought the legal challenge will collect statutory attorneys fees from the state that enacted the provision in the amount of hundreds of thousands of dollars."[112]

This has unfortunately come to be known as the "timing argument." Bopp then proceeded to add a last point, which we dub "the sky is falling" argument. He stated that perhaps a loss would allow the proabortion members of the Supreme Court to rewrite Roe on a more substantial foundation than the "right to privacy" that Blackmun derived from the "due process" clause of our Constitution. Indeed, it was this last argument that resonated with many of the rank-and-file Right to Life leaders around the country.

Discounting number four, because the fear of losing has not stopped NRLC from engaging in long and extended court battles in the past. They lost the initial Partial Birth Abortion Ban at the state level. They went to Congress and fought it again at a federal level, this time to victory. The loss at a state level helped induce Congress to act.

The Sky is Falling Argument

Let's examine these arguments. We begin in reverse order because the number one objection to Personhood continues to be fear of what *might* happen if we were to aggressively pursue Personhood as a public policy objective.

Fear is a tremendous motivator. The Bible tells us that fear is not from God. In contrast, God's gift is reason and a "sound mind" (see 2 Timothy 1:7 KJV). The God-given response that should be evidenced by prolife leadership at both the national and state levels is to sit down and count the costs of waging war for the hearts and minds of the culture. It is to prudently apply wisdom in a well-reasoned anticipation of a genuine advance in public policy and law.

It is to display a level of Christian faith and courage that is founded upon truth and pursued diligently and without compromise. It is to join with the prolife saints of every century of Church history to speak the truth in love and to give an answer for the hope within us— toward the end that we would see a sanctity-of-life ethic preserved in our culture and during our time in history.

Our experience in Georgia over the last decade is that it is easier to invoke moral cowardice by appealing to a spirit of fear than it is to inspire courage to stand alone for righteousness' sake. Yet when we do stand with biblical courage and the moral certitude of our position, God works on our behalf, empowering us to triumph, both politically and legislatively.

Indeed, the undisputed empirical data from Georgia has challenged the prolife movement nationally to reconsider its effectiveness in light of this ancient strategy.[113] Since changing to a Personhood strategy in 2001, GRTL has progressed from being near the bottom in the nation in enacting prolife law to being ranked the eighth most prolife state in the nation in 2010, according to Americans United for Life.[114] Over half of *all* Georgia's elected officials hold the position that abortion should be illegal except in cases in which the mother's life is in danger *and* only after both the mother and child have been treated equally in terms of the attempt to preserve life.

In 2009 the Georgia State GOP adopted the Personhood amendment as a statewide resolution, and in the 2010 Republican gubernatorial primary six of the seven candidates for governor supported the personhood amendment to the state constitution. The candidate who ultimately won via runoff election defeated the only non-Personhood candidate; she was a "conservative prolifer" with rape and incest exceptions. Surprisingly, Sarah Palin, who is adamant that she would not allow abortion in those specific cases, endorsed this candidate.[115] In July of 2010 Georgia became the first state in the nation, in a nonbinding straw poll (46 counties), to have its voters approve a "Human Life Amendment" question. The average yes vote on the Republican primary ballot was 75% and on the Democrat primary ballot 72%.[116] In November 2010, during the general election, all nine statewide constitutional offices were won by candidates who support a "no exceptions" position on abortion and the call for a Personhood amendment to our state constitution.

Obviously, we have been successful at the public policy level in educating the general public and moving our voters to favor Personhood. We have been successful at a political level by the sheer number of politicians who have "upgraded" their former "rape and incest" positions to reflect the changing face of 21st century issues. We have been successful at the legislative level in passing most of the laws regulating abortion that have been recommended by NRLC— so much so that, when asked where we should go from here, prolife leaders responded by saying that we should go back and tighten up our existing language.[117] We have also succeeded in moving our legislature into the 21st century; in 2009 Georgia became the first state in the nation to pass an "embryo adoption" bill.

Personhood has seen dramatic success in Georgia over the last decade. Yet each victory has the critics "explaining away" our success. We at GRTL allege that the same results can be experienced, over time, by any state willing to take a biblical stand.

Unfortunately, a spirit of fear responds "That might be well for Georgia in the deep South, but that will never work in my state." Fear *always* "snatches defeat from the jaws of victory" because it never attempts anything based on well-reasoned, faithful actions. President Theodore Roosevelt stated it this way:

> It is not the critic who counts; not the man who points out how the strong man stumbles, or where the doer of deeds could have done them better. The credit belongs to the man who is actually in the arena, whose face is marred by dust and sweat and blood; who strives valiantly; who errs,

who comes short again and again, because there is no effort without error and shortcoming; but who does actually strive to do the deeds; who knows great enthusiasms, the great devotions; who spends himself in a worthy cause; who at the best knows in the end the triumph of high achievement, and who at the worst, if he fails, at least fails while daring greatly, so that his place shall never be with those cold and timid souls who neither know victory nor defeat.[118]

Kingmakers v. Standard Bearers

A large portion of this fear of action can be attributed to the desire of prolife leaders to be "king-makers" rather than "standard-bearers." To be a "king-maker" you must preserve access to the corridors of power, and that entails compromise and accommodation. To be a "standard-bearer," on the other hand, one must act without compromise and remain faithful regardless of the political realities or circumstances.

Mother Teresa put it this way: "God doesn't require us to succeed; he only requires that you try."[119] On another occasion she restated her axiom as follows: "I do not pray for success, I ask for faithfulness."[120] Fear of loss should never dictate a Christian organization's moral position, political alliances, legislative objectives, or public policy debates. To reiterate the salient point: Fear is *not* from God. If we are *not* a Christian-based organization, then nothing needs to change, but if we *are* (GRTL is faith-based according to our bylaws), then we, as Christian prolife leaders, need to begin acting like it.

The Bible is clear that eternal judgment is not exclusively reserved for murderers, the sexually immoral, liars, and idolaters, but that it will also include those who are "cowardly and faithless" (Revelation 21:8). I am not suggesting that every national prolife leader who admonishes caution, prudence, or counting the cost is in danger of losing his or her immortal soul. I am merely pointing out that there is a sin that causes righteous men to stumble, and in so doing to accomplish far less than they might have accomplished if encouraged to uphold a biblical standard.

A wise man once said, "We will not be judged by God for what we have accomplished, but rather, we will be judged by what we have accomplished compared to what we COULD have accomplished"[121] had we responded biblically. Mr. Gualberto Garcia Jones, director of Personhood Colorado, has this to say in his article titled "Prudence And Moral Clarity In The Quest For Personhood": "The close relationship between the social conscience and representative democracy is at the heart of American and world history. Behind every major twist and turn of history there is a social movement driven not by legal subterfuge and political compromise but unabashed truth, courage, and clarity."[122]

Moral courage and the truth of Personhood as a 21st-century strategy will be necessary if we desire to see the same level of victory in prolife endeavors as the Church has experienced in history—and as we have experienced in Georgia—solely by God's grace to His glory.

Legal Defense of Personhood Amendment

In 2007 Georgia Right to Life (GRTL) introduced the nation's first Personhood legislation at a state level. It was a Human Life Amendment to the state constitution. GRTL's legal efforts were defended, at the time, by Atty. Robert Muise of Thomas More Law Center. Responding to Bopp's attack on our efforts, Muise posted a rebuttal calling for immediate support of a legal strategy that would promote a paramount human life amendment at a state level. He argued on two primary levels:

The proposed constitutional amendment would provide the opportunity for the case to be made that human life begins at conception. . . . Additionally, the proposed constitutional amendment explicitly affirms, as a matter of state law, that "Personhood" attaches at the moment of fertilization. It is a well-established principle of law that States possess the right to adapt their own constitutions with rights more expansive than those conferred by the federal constitution. See Prunyard Shopping Ctr. v. Robins, 447 U.S. 74, 81 (1980) ("affirming "the authority of the State to exercise its police power [and] its sovereign right to adopt in its own Constitution individual liberties more expansive that those conferred by the Federal Constitution").[123]

In 2008 Muise was invited to the *115 Forum*, a prestigious prolife forum that meets by invitation only in the nation's capital—a virtual "Who's who?" of national prolife leadership. He was scheduled to engage in a one-hour debate with attorney James Bopp Jr., who took issue with the Personhood strategy.[124] Many of the nation's top prolife leaders were present for the debate, and many of the groups were exposed to the Personhood strategy for the first time. Several of the leaders expressed to me their personal disappointment with Mr. Bopp's arguments, which they found to be less than persuasive. Evidently they were expecting an ironclad critique of Personhood from a legal perspective and were disappointed by the criticisms of Personhood, more specifically focused on the timing argument.

The Timing Argument

The overall response from most of the mainline leadership could fairly be described as taking to heart Bopp's admonition "first do no harm." They were responding to the "sky is falling" argument based on fear of setting the prolife movement backward, especially if Roe were to be challenged under the current makeup of the Court: "The timing is not right because we do not have the necessary votes on the Court."

Joining Bopp was National Right to Life Committee (NRLC). This was in fact NRLC's very entrenched response, which is not surprising in that Mr. Bopp is the organization's legal counsel. What is interesting is that 18 months later, with *no* changes at the Supreme Court level, NRLC abruptly reversed its position regarding the timeliness and outcome of challenging Roe and supported just such an exercise.

The reality is that the "sky is falling" argument has also been applied to each of the major cases that has come before the Court since 1973. As with *Casey* and *Gonzales*, it is possible that the 2010 Nebraska fetal pain law will be challenged and work its way through the federal court system. There it would be feasible, though admittedly less than likely, for the courts to rewrite Roe upon a more substantial legal foundation, thereby doing immeasurable harm to the movement nationally. This hasn't happened. Must we be immobilized by fear when organizations such as Georgia Right to Life have demonstrated the wisdom of using the Personhood strategy to accomplish gains in every political, legislative, and public policy arena?

Since 2008 many other national prolife law firms and groups have joined forces to defend a timely challenge to Roe as a viable legal strategy.[125] In fact, in the spring of 2010 National Right to Life Committee reversed a policy of waiting until the "timing was right" before introducing its newest challenge to Roe by crafting and passing the "The Pain-Capable Unborn Child Protection Act"[126] in Nebraska.

Were they afraid that Mr. Bopp's argument that "the sky is falling" would apply to their efforts? Apparently not. Mrs. Mary Balch, state legislative director for NRLC, in the spring of 2010 stated: "I think National Right to Life wants to see something go to the Supreme Court that would provide more protection to the unborn child."[127] Obviously the supporters hope that Supreme Court justice Anthony

Kennedy will continue to side with the Roberts' court and provide the swing vote to place further limits on abortion, knowing that this would provide yet another opportunity to return Roe to the states. This was true of the last two NRLC cases: *Casey v. Planned Parenthood* and *Gonzales v. Carhart*. In each instance, although the "sky is falling" argument was in play, the case was still construed to challenge Roe as part of a well-calculated risk.

The Supreme Court Will Not Hear the Case

This is what I affectionately call the "crystal ball" argument. In truth, no one knows what the Supreme Court might do. No prolife legal entity has a crystal ball with which it can categorically predict the future, and yet this has not stopped them from making their predictions of doom and gloom.

Several factors shed new light on the question of the Supreme Court's willingness to hear a case that might reverse Roe, thereby opening the door for states to enact their own recognition of Personhood in their constitutions and statutes.

The first focuses its attention on Justice Anthony Kennedy's perceived position as casting the swing vote in favor of reversing Roe. It has been noted that, since Chief Justice Roberts was appointed, Kennedy has voted with the conservative majority the greater part of the time. University of Georgia law professor Randy Beck, a former aid of Justice Kennedy, visited the GRTL offices during the summer of 2010 with the intent of promoting a ban on abortion that he suggested would appeal to Justice Kennedy's most recent logic in his writing the majority opinion for the Gonzales v. Carhart case. Beck had this to say: "Justice Kennedy explained [that] . . . by common understanding and scientific terminology, a fetus is a living organism while within the womb, whether or not it is viable outside the womb."[128] He further claimed that Kennedy made some foundational assumptions in Carhart "when Justice Kennedy recognized in his *Stenberg* dissent that the state interest in protecting dependent human life applies likewise to the life of a fetus."[129]

Justice Kennedy himself, writing in his dissent in the Stenberg case, stated the following: "A State may take measures to ensure the medical profession and its members are viewed as healers, sustained by a compassionate and rigorous ethic and cognizant of the dignity and value of human life, even life which cannot survive without the assistance of others."[130] Beck concludes that "The Court's unanimity on these points gives hope that it may be willing to take up the largely neglected question of the rationale for the viability rule, one important component in this highly visible segment of the Court's constitutional jurisprudence."[131] All of this to say that a former law clerk for Justice Kennedy and a well-respected professor of law at the University of Georgia believes that a case involving an egress of viability would be the most effective means of presenting Justice Kennedy with a case that he might conceivably use to reverse Roe and return the issue to the states. National Right to Life now agrees and hope that a challenge of the Nebraska Pain-Capable Unborn Child Protection Act is just such a case.[132]

A second factor that would lead us to hope that now is the time for the Court to reverse Roe is that year after year polling has empirically shown that the majority of the nation now considers itself prolife.[133] For the last two years, national polling companies have confirmed that Americans have become much more assured of their prolife positions.

In Georgia, our experience with the Personhood strategy has resulted in a dramatic shift in public opinion. During the week of November 2–4, 2006, Strategic Vision, a national polling company, conducted a survey of 800 voters, of whom they asked a number of questions, one of which related to *Roe v. Wade*. The margin of sampling error is ±3 percentage points. The question: "Would you like to see the United States Supreme Court overturn the Roe v. Wade decision that makes abortions legal in the United States?" 57% said yes. During that period the same question was asked in several other very strong prolife states, with a much lower favorable response. The yes responses are as follows: Washington 26%, Pennsylvania 33%, Michigan 35%, New Jersey 35%, Wisconsin 37%, and Florida 38%. At the time of the poll, and among the ten states that were polled, Georgia polled 19 percentage points above the next *nearest* state.[134] It is not my intention to continue to hype our prolife accomplishments in Georgia; it is my intent to challenge our detractors who said a decade ago that our objectives were imprudent, untimely, and dangerous to the cause. You be the judge.

Finally, what would be the outcome of the untimely removal or death of one of the four presumably prolife justices on the Supreme Court? President Obama would logically appoint a liberal, pro-culture of death justice, and we would be counseled to "wait" another thirty years (another generation) before we could hope for a realignment in our favor. This is unimaginable. If such a thing occurs, using the logic of the prevailing prolife legal opinion, we as a movement might as well pack our bags and go home. The only suggested strategy is the same tired refrain: "Fence abortion through incremental regulation." By the time the courts would conceivably be rebalanced, three more decades would have passed, and public opinion and the culture of death would have been set in concrete.

Summary

The policy for a post-human future is being debated today. We, as a movement, are largely silent. Today's prolife leaders have one answer to question of "Is it time to re-visit Personhood as an effective prolife strategy?" Their answer is "Wait! Wait until all of the political and judicial stars line up."

Delaying a Personhood strategy is simply not an option. The future waits for no man.

Chapter 7

Personhood: How Can I Start the Process in My State?

Power concedes nothing without a demand. It never did and it never will. Find out just what any people will quietly submit to and you have found out the exact measure of injustice and wrong which will be imposed upon them, and these will continue till they are resisted with either words or blows, or both. The limits of tyrants are prescribed by the endurance of those whom they oppress.

Abolitionist Frederick Douglas

We are cleaning house and in order to clean house the one thing we need is a good broom. Initiatives and referendum are good brooms.

President Woodrow Wilson

Start by Engaging in the Political and Legislative Process

In Romans 13:1 God reminds us that He is the source of all government: "Let every person be subject to the governing authorities. For there is no authority except from God, and those that exist have been instituted by God." This is a profound truth that is nevertheless misunderstood by many professing Christians, particularly within the American Church. Paul was reminding the Church in Rome, in the first century, that God was the actual author of the Roman Republic and that it served at His pleasure for the purpose of protecting the righteous and punishing the wicked with the power of the sword.

Let us contrast the biblical view to the neo-pagan concept of utilitarianism. Utilitarian government states its purpose as "the greatest good for the greatest number." This concept is found no where in the biblical text. Government is defined biblically as being tasked with defending the innocent, the weak and the helpless, against those stronger who seek to harm them. I find it ironic that paraplegic Christopher Reeve appeared before the Senate Health, Education, Labor and Pensions Committee, the committee overseeing cloning and destructive embryonic stem cell research, bringing testimony that would have supported his own death. "Today 100 million Americans suffer from serious or currently incurable diseases. 54 million Americans are disabled. Our government is supposed to do the greatest good for the greatest number of people..." What Christopher Reeve fails to deduce is that a utilitarian government would simply have reduced our population by 154 million thereby reducing the healthcare expense of treating those whose utility to the greater number no longer exists. According to his utilitarian philosophy of government he should have never received treatment. Nazi Germany implemented this form of government and a quarter of a million people were put to death. A Washington Times article, November 23, 2008, reported the following:

"Adolf Hitler in the late 1930's started the T4 Aktion (Action) program, named after the main office's address at Tiergartenstrasse 4 in Berlin, to exterminate 'useless eaters', babies born with disabilities. When any baby was born in Germany, the attending nurse had to note any indication of disability and immediately notify T4 officials - a team of physicians, politicians and military leaders. In October 1939 Hitler issued a directive allowing physicians to grant a 'mercy death' to "patients considered incurable according to the best available human judgment of their state of health.

Thereafter, the program expanded to include older children and adults with disabilities, and anyone anywhere in the Third Reich was subject to execution who was blind, deaf, senile, retarded, or had any significant neurological condition, encephalitis, epilepsy, muscular spasticity or paralysis. Six killing centers were eventually established, and an estimated quarter-million people with disabilities were executed."

In Nazi Germany government was reduced to a utilitarian approach to human life. Human life can be quantified and qualified according to the needs of the greatest number. An individual human life becomes a commodity, some have value and some do not. Under President Obama's healthcare plan "quality of life" scores are being used to rate those who are entitled to receive treatment and those who do not score high enough. Many different medical factors are used to determine your score. If you walk with a limp, a half of a point is deducted from your score. This is just one example of many which shows why Christians should be engaged in politics, lest we lose our biblical foundation completely.

Paul's Roman Republic lasted a little over two hundred years before it succumbed to becoming an empire, later falling into decay.

From the first century to the present, governments have both been raised up and displaced by God. Around 1776 God raised up a unique form of government in the American colonies—a government that derived its authority from "the consent of the governed,"[135] a "government of the people, by the people and for the people,"[136] a government known as a constitutional republic.

By design, our government requires continuous input from the people to function within its proper bounds. Without citizen participation this form of government will ultimately devolve into either a plutocracy—government of, by, and for the wealthiest class (both Democratic and Republican), or an oligarchy of elite rulers (career politicians ruling an empire), or the totalitarian rule of a highly charismatic individual (like Hitler). Each of these excesses could conceivably implement a utilitarian regime. In order to limit these excesses, powers are granted to the governed.

This is where many American Christians fall off the wagon: They refuse to engage the political obligations that God has placed upon every American believer by virtue of the fact that He gave this unique gift to our country. He raised up a constitutional republic and instructs us to use it wisely. By abdicating the political and governmental field of battle, we fly in the face of the prevenient grace of God. We say to Him, "We don't care that the form of government you gave us requires our participation; we choose instead to focus on our religious duties. After all, politics is no place for a Christian."

As our Lord Jesus reminded us, "You are the salt of the earth, but if salt has lost its taste, how shall its saltiness be restored? It is no longer good for anything except to be thrown out and trampled under people's feet" (Matthew 5:13). A Christian's duty before God in respect to civil government and culture is to act as a preservative, lest God come and find us tasteless and cast us out. Without the preserving influence of Christians in the political realm, government will devolve and decay, and many will suffer.

Uniting Our Voices for Change

The process of changing the laws or constitutions of the various states resides in two types of governmental processes— one relatively simple compared to the other. Both employ direct citizen action.

The first is the ballot initiative or referendum process, whereby a proposal, a new law, or a constitutional amendment may be placed on the ballot by a petition initiated by a group of motivated citizens. By means of petitioning and gathering a defined number of signatures, a point of law bypasses the normal legislative process and is put directly in front of the voters. There are currently twenty-four states allowing for some form of ballot initiative.

The second is a legislative measure or proposition, a proposal placed on the ballot by the legislature. All states permit legislative measures, and all except Delaware require constitutional amendments to be approved by the voters at large.

To determine whether your state allows for a ballot initiative, please go online to http://www.iandrinstitute.org/statewide_i&r.htm.

The Initiative and Referendum Process

In 1898 South Dakota became the first state to adopt the statewide initiative process. South Dakotans were led by a Catholic priest, Father Robert W. Haire, who volunteered with the underground railroad and later worked for women's suffrage. From the outset the initiative and referendum process arose from the people's dissatisfaction with the political party system and its inability to effectively address the concerns of minority interests opposed to the powerful, apolitical elite. Sadly, Father Haire was stripped of his priestly privileges by his bishop, Martin Marty, who deemed him to be too political.

The initiative and referendum process flowered in the West, where political elites were less entrenched and where the populist belief was strongest that the people should rule the elected and not the elected rule the people. In the South and East a strong racist current prevented the initiative process from being adopted: in the South on the basis of a perceived fear of "negro domination," and in the East because of fear of "Irish-Catholic voting blocs."

By 1918 twenty-four states had adopted the initiative and referendum process. Over the next 70 years the number of initiative and referendum states has remained the same; there are still twenty-four states in which the initiative process is available.

Benefits of the Initiative and Referendum Process

The initiative and referendum process presents voters with an opportunity to vote on issues when political parties refuse to advocate for them or are willing to do so only half-heartedly. This process also provides voters with a guarantee that the law will reflect their point of view—a guarantee that is never possible with elected politicians. As Grover Norquist, president of Americans for Tax Reform, once stated sarcastically: "One big difference between initiatives and elected representatives is that initiatives do not change their minds once you vote them in."

The initiative and referendum process has been used as a way to limit government when the legislature has not been willing to limit itself. For example, it has been used to adopt term limits, lower property taxes, impose balanced budgets, and require votes of the people before tax increases can be adopted.

This process has also been used to extend rights to politically powerless groups. Examples of this are granting women the right to vote, eliminating poll taxes, and imposing regulations on the powerful abortion industry.

The common denominator for recourse to the initiative process is that, for whatever reason, the legislature is unwilling or unable to bring about a legislative change.

Accessibility to Law Making

The initiative and referendum process takes the procedural technicalities of lawmaking out of the equation. Typically, initiatives are written and advocated by nonprofessionals who simply have a passion for a particular issue. With some minimal help in drafting (sometimes available from the state itself, but more often from an organization with proper resources), any citizen can introduce and circulate a petition for a constitutional amendment. If enough signatures are gathered, the language conceived around a kitchen table can make its way to the ballot of every single voter.

Voter Participation

While politics is the art of compromise, initiatives are the standard bearers of principle. Initiatives often present a black and white issue, a yes or no question.

The choice of a political candidate involves the weighing of a myriad of often-conflicting issues and opinions, and it involves placing trust in politicians. The initiative and referendum process, on the other hand, presents a clear issue: abortion, yes or no; homosexual marriage, yes or no; or the same question for term limits, property tax increases, etc. In a climate in which the rates of unaffiliated voters are climbing, when voters feel as though they cannot trust either party to represent their views, the initiative and referendum process has statistically proven to bring 3-5% more voters to the polls to voice their opinion and to directly make law.

Education

Abortion is the perfect example of how the initiative and referendum process can serve as a catalyst for education. The sanctity of life is an issue on which a majority of Americans agree; still, the majority of America would allow Roe v. Wade to continue, in part because the abortion industry spends millions of dollars annually spreading misinformation, with most professional associations parroting the abortionists' propaganda. Universities are almost universally centers of proabortion indoctrination, as are the press and mainstream culture icons.

From the populist movements that demanded just labor laws and women's suffrage to the modern prolife movement, the initiative process has proven itself to be an effective way for the have-nots to persistently push for laws that the mainstream political process, indebted to the abortion industry, would never allow to come to a vote. In Colorado, for example, the state legislature and governorship have been under Democratic control at least from 2006 to 2010. The options for prolife lawmaking were the following: (1) try to get Democrats to vote on a principled prolife measure in the legislature (this has never happened since Roe v. Wade); (2) try to work on a compromise law that allows for abortion to continue being legal albeit under more restricted conditions; and (3) use the initiative process to present the voters directly with a law that represents exactly what the activists desire. In fact, the Colorado Catholic Conference attempted to get the Democrat- controlled legislature to consider an Unborn Victims of Violence Act, which excluded any prosecution for abortions and which defined an unborn child as a human being after 16 weeks of development. Even though this law was hardly prolife, it was killed in committee and never made a single headline.

On the other hand, the Personhood amendment, backed by little more than $20,000, was able to energize prolifers in Colorado to go directly to the people, talking face to face with more than a million constituents in the process of gathering the signatures necessary to get on the ballot. Once on the ballot, the amendment made local, state, and national news, providing opportunity for a discussion that was framed in terms and language chosen by the proponents of the measure.

The Initiative Process Enhances Education

Following are some observations that demonstrate how the initiative process is able to enhance our educational message:

1. The signature process is a natural educational procedure that requires face-to-face conversations.
2. Because the prolife movement is a moral rather than a purely political movement, it enjoys access to networks of churches and family organizations that make coordination and outreach during the campaigns incredibly cost effective and personal.
3. Initiatives are inherently offensive (as opposed to defensive).

Because many state constitutions can be amended by a simple majority vote of the people, the constitutional initiative is ideal for wiping the slate clean. Initiatives require the defenders of the status quo to put everything on the line. Initiative votes are like allowing a challenger a shot at the world title every time there is a vote.

4. Initiatives are an ideal fit for grass roots organizations. After clearing away language technicalities, there is little or nothing that the abortion monopoly can do to silence a vigorous debate of the issue.

5. History shows that initiatives and referendums have been used to educate not only the public but also the politicians. By providing a direct vote on a very specific question, politicians get a clear sense of the importance of that detailed issue. In Colorado, which became a blue state in the last five years, now politicians know that 30% of the population believes preborn children are persons. They now understand that taking a position allowing for rape and incest exceptions or one allowing early abortions will jeopardize the support of 30% of the voting bloc. A candidate for statewide office in Colorado in 2010 is a prime example. Early in his campaign for the U.S. Senate, he voiced his support for a no-exceptions position. Later, when he came under attack from proabortion Democrats, he flip-flopped and lost the support of his base. He also lost his election by a very narrow margin.[137]

How Do I Begin a Ballot Initiative in My State?

Without question, my advice would be for you to contact PersonhoodUSA (see Appendix 3). Keith Mason, Cal Zastrow, and Gualberto Jones have worked with a number of states in helping to launch a ballot initiative effort. They can answer your questions and provide helpful direction and are an all-around resource, both legally and organizationally. They are underfunded and overworked, but I firmly believe that their tireless efforts will change the course of U.S. history.

Legislative Process

The initiative and referendum process is legal, in some form, in twenty-four states. The legislative proposition, on the other hand, is legal in all fifty. In many states a super majority or 66% of both chambers of the legislature must vote in order to place a constitutional amendment before the voters. This is a substantial hurdle to overcome—after which the people must still affirm the issue by majority vote. This long and involved process requires that a significant portion of the voting public put pressure on their elected officials to legislatively place the question on the general election ballot. This requires an informed and motivated electorate. There are a number of concrete steps that can be taken in any state that wishes to shape public opinion and influence public policy in this way.

Organize

Checkout the local National Right to Life affiliate in your state, you might find that they are very welcoming. If they are not, join a statewide prolife organization that supports Personhood; if one does not exist, form your own. Use the power of social networking to set a date and advertise the formation of a statewide steering committee to promote Personhood. If that objective seems too intimidating, start at a county or city level and then join other locales to form a statewide network.

Educate Yourself

Avail yourselves of the educational resources that are listed in Appendix 3. Be knowledgeable about the issues and be prepared to answer those who initially oppose your efforts. Do so in a gracious and humble manner, bearing in mind our own experience at GRTL that even the strongest opponents can be won over by faithful perseverance and a victorious outcome. Truth will win out, but it can take time.

Educate Others

Schedule as many speaking engagements as you can. Share the message of Personhood in churches, civic groups, political party gatherings, and throughout the editorial pages of your local media. It's essential for you to understand that to skip this step and jump immediately to the legislative process is to act out of order. If you proceed in this way, I can guarantee that you'll be frustrated and disappointed in the outcome. Remember to place a priority on education before moving on to political action and finally to legislation.

Engage in Political Action

Form both a state and a federal Political Action Committee (PAC). A PAC's sole purpose is to influence the election or defeat of a particular candidate or issue. The legal and reporting requirements are relatively simple but vary from state to state. Churches cannot associate with a PAC when it promotes the election or defeat of a certain candidate, but they can advocate for or against a particular issue. Since the primary purpose of the PAC will be to elect pro-Personhood candidates, it's vitally important that the PAC include the following tenets in its bylaws:

- Establish a set of endorsement criteria based on Personhood (e.g., Do not permit a prolife candidate to claim a rape or incest exception. They must agree that abortion is legal only to save the life of the mother AND only when both mother and child are treated. Advocacy for a pro-Personhood amendment). GRTL publishes a 20-page position paper[138] on all the current issues (www.grtl.org). Endorsed candidates must agree 100% with our position (a radical notion) *and* must sign a Candidate Affirmation form[139] in order to be included in the "white list" (see bullet point below). We added language this year that requires them to work within the party establishment to promote our sponsored legislation.

- Publish a "white list," including *only* those candidates who are 100% with you. This forces all so-called "prolife" politicians to "upgrade" their prolife positions in light of 21st-century issues. Encourage your base to publicly question those whose names do not appear on the white list.

- Seek local party support for Personhood at a state level (e.g.,, county, district and state Personhood resolutions). Make the issue a plank of the state party platform.

- Place as phone call to the Chairman of the local parties in your county. Request that the local county parties place the question on their ballots during the primary. This constitutes a nonbinding poll that cannot be ignored by local politicians.

- Purchase and deploy Campaign Tracker from PersonhoodUSA. This one piece of software will immediately leverage your efforts and encourage others to become politically active, if in no other way than to pen a letter to the editors of local papers.

Legislate

Once you achieve success at the PAC level—and you will—you're ready to begin offering pro-Personhood legislation. It isn't necessary to have a majority of Personhood-endorsed candidates because many of the "rape and incest" prolifers will vote with you on the bill. It is important to understand some of the nuances of evaluating and promoting Personhood bills:

- All legislation must be consistent with a Personhood amendment.
- All legislation is incremental (e.g.,, state Personhood amendment, ban on abortion, etc.). We acknowledge that a state Personhood amendment is considered an incremental step toward achieving the final victory of a Constitutional amendment at a federal level. 33 states need to pass a state amendment before we can expect to achieve our primary objective at a federal level.
- Expand beyond the abortion issue and offer bills that emphasize Personhood in other areas (destructive stem cell research, IVF, end of life issues, etc.).
- Reject all legislation that says "and then you can kill the baby" or "nothing in this bill shall be construed to challenge Roe." Don't feed the monster of misguided legal positivism.
- Many potential allies have come out against state Personhood amendments because its passage at a state level would leave some states without Personhood protection. They believe that the only proper Personhood strategy should be to pursue the objective at a federal level *only*. They fail to realize that this strategy has been in place the last four decades. It leads to the unsatisfactory conclusion that "if we can't save all, we shouldn't save any."
- Another problem arises when Personhood allies carry their enthusiasm to save all children, too far. They fail to apply a level of critical thinking to their well intentioned opposition to compromise. For example, state legislation that would ban destructive stem cell research would save 100% of a class of human beings, those fertilized in vitro. (A "class of human life" is not an attempt to demean human life. I use the term to denote a very defined and legally recognized segment of life that is being affirmatively protected by law.) Preserving

the life of one class of humans is *not* the equivalent of saying "and then you can kill the rest." Why wouldn't we support a state level bill that saves 100% of a class of human life, for example, outlawing selective reduction thereby preventing the death of "excess" children implanted during infertility treatments? This becomes an important point because many Personhood supporters have gone too far to the extreme and have denounced perfectly good bills that would have saved 100% of a class of human life facing death at the hands of an abortionist. Let me explain. How many of us would be for a complete abortion ban without any exceptions? Most of us I am sure. Follow the logic. The problem is that, using this flawed logic, we have just agreed to killing babies who are not covered by a complete abortion ban, such as, children being destroyed through embryonic stem cell research—aren't they deserving of protection? Using this logic all purists should oppose any legislation other than a Personhood Amendment which protects ALL human life. Using this flawed logic they should oppose a complete ban on abortion. *The problem rests in the fact that we are so focused on abortion as the only sanctity of life issue that we fail to see the larger picture.* A ban on abortion that only saves children 20 weeks or older, saves 100% of that class of human life. A ban on abortion coinciding with a fetal heartbeat is better and saves more of a class of human life. A ban on abortion in cases of gender or racial discrimination save 100% of that class of human life. No where does the logic imply "that then you can kill the other babies, the elderly, the infirm or children in a cryopreserved state." Make no mistake, I am for a complete ban on abortion because it saves 100% of a class of human life . . . but that class only represents children being threatened with death at the hands of an abortionist and by definition is only an incremental step in protecting all innocent human life.

- Regulating to prevent killing isn't immoral or anti-Personhood when its goal will protect a "Personhood class." We base this on Proverbs 24:11, "Rescue those who are being taken away to death; hold back those who are stumbling to the slaughter." This biblical principle allows for "saving some, when it is not possible to save all", as long as, we do not include language that defines, and then executes, a class of human life by lawful edict. These types of legislation can be written in such a way as to remove any implication that all human classes NOT covered by the bill are "less than human." Unfortunately, many of these type bills, do contain flawed language and should be rejected.

In a state in which ballot initiatives are not available, be prepared for a long process. In Georgia we began by seeing almost immediate success at a PAC level. Legislative success started with a trickle—a trickle that reached flood stage over the course of ten years. Political favor can wax and wane like the weather. In the Georgia House, like many other state legislatures, all decision making and control comes down to one person, the Speaker of the House. If he or she opposes our efforts, there is not much we can do except resort to political action. Let me repeat, if you encounter opposition, fall back on political action. Let me say it again; do not succumb to the siren call of accessed based politics, false promises or *quid pro quo* politics—take them on and force them out! You will win in the end. It's imperative to recognize that in politics we have no eternal friends or perpetual enemies but only enduring interests.

Summary
Every person has a right to life, and every citizen has a voice to speak for those who cannot speak for themselves. We have a form of government granted by God that allows our voices to be heard. Our collective voices can—and should—change the course of history.

Chapter 8

Personhood: The Battle is the Lord's

Were not the Ethiopians and the Lubim an immense army with very many chariots and horsemen? Yet because you relied on the LORD, He delivered them into your hand. For the eyes of the LORD move to and fro throughout the earth that He may strongly support those whose heart is completely His.

2 Chronicles 16:9 (NASB)

Why do you break the commandments of the LORD, so that you cannot prosper? Because you have forsaken the LORD, he has forsaken you.

2 Chronicles 24:20

I am the Lord. I have spoken; it shall come to pass; I will do it. I will not go back; I will not spare; I will not relent; according to your ways and your deeds you will be judged, declares the Lord God.

Ezekiel 24:14

For kingship belongs to the LORD, and he rules over the nations.

Psalm 22:28

The Battle Is the Lord's

In Ephesians 6:12 Paul points out that our struggle as Christians is ultimately not with people but against powerful spiritual beings. Can anyone deny that the demonic forces that encouraged child sacrifice in the Old Testament are actively promoting the same evil agenda in our day? I praise God for the prolife victories He has decreed for Georgia. Yes, you heard me correctly . . . *decreed!* Our God is a power to be reckoned with, even when talking political strategy and public discourse. He claims to be seated on a throne, ruling the nations from on high (Colossians 3:1). When confronted by political and governmental opposition to God's revealed will, the psalmist made this response: "He who sits in the heavens laughs; the LORD holds them in derision (Psalm 2:4). In our day, this same Lord warns our President, our Justices, our Congressmen, and our local state officials: "Now therefore, O kings, be wise; be warned, O rulers of the earth. Serve the LORD with fear, and rejoice with trembling. Kiss the Son, lest he be angry, and you perish in the way, for his wrath is quickly kindled" (verses 10–12). Is it somehow wrong to believe that God has the power to remove those politicians and judges who oppose Him, while establishing those who honor Him and His Word?

In Georgia we have experienced multiple occasions in which a powerful political opponent has been removed from office by the hand of God. Our GRTL staff prays regularly that God would work in situations where political leaders oppose prolife efforts. We ask God to "change their hearts or change their locations." God has done both. He has removed leaders from power, and he has turned former enemies into allies. Perhaps the most amazing account of conversion from an active pro-abortion politician to an equally active prolife advocate is former Georgia Governor Zell Miller. For years, first as Lieutenant Governor and later as Governor, he opposed our legislation and thwarted our efforts to protect the innocent. His two term opposition as Governor caused our prolife caucus members to despair of ever seeing meaningful prolife legislation. Upon the unexpected death of Republican U.S. Senator Paul Coverdell (July 18, 2000), our newly elected pro-abortion Democratic Governor Roy Barnes appointed former Governor Zell Miller to finish out the term of Senator Coverdell. We steeled ourselves for the worst. Imagine our surprise when Senator Miller ardently defended the sanctity of life. His conversion to a prolife position was national news. Beyond daily prayer for our government officials, what other factors contributed to his change of heart? It was the simple act of being handed an ultrasound picture of his first grandchild. Suddenly all the rhetoric of "choice" and a "right to privacy" was cast to the wind as he gazed with the loving eyes of a grandfather onto the small form of his pre-born granddaughter. We were privileged to have Senator Miller as the keynote speaker for our annual fund-raising banquet. I watched in awe as Senator Miller entered the ballroom of the event. The first person to greet him was Georgia State House Representative James Mills, leader of our prolife caucus. Rep. Mills extended his hand to greet his former adversary and instead of griping his hand, Senator Miller engulfed him an embrace, holding Rep Mills for a full minute as he whispered his apologizes in a very personal manner. Rep. Mills was overcome with emotion, with tears streaming down his cheeks, he nodded his personal forgiveness to a man that had worked from a position of great political power to undo all of our prolife legislation. From the podium, Senator Miller apologized for his opposition and pledged to do what he could to undo the harm which weighed on his conscience. This he did . . . and more!

God has also removed those who had hardened their hearts, so that they are no longer a hindrance.[140]

I doubt any Christian would deny that God has the power to do as He pleases. What, then, prevents him from acting to remove the evil men and women that blight our land? Did God intervene to prevent David from engaging Goliath? I firmly believe that He is looking for the faithful few who will, by faith and in prayer, stand boldly against the "giants in the land," trusting in His promise that He will never leave us or forsake us. Without faith, we know, it is impossible to please God (Hebrews 11:6). All we need is a desire to be obedient to His commands and faithful in our perseverance. The battle is the Lord's.

Personhood Will Not Work in My State

I am well aware that my words appear to many to be too spiritual to be of any earthy good. Yet this is precisely what the Church has experienced in many cultures over many centuries. Prolife victories are assured when God's providence manifests itself in and through our efforts. To say that Personhood "will not work in my state" is true only if Christianity itself "will not work." Our God is certainly able to engineer victory for His people.

"My state is too liberal." "A Personhood strategy is too radical; it will never work in my state!" I tend to agree with theologian G. K. Chesterton that "Christianity has not been tried and found wanting; it has been found difficult and not tried." One can never know what *can* be accomplished in a state (or nation, for that matter) until one tries. Take, for instance, the liberal, proabortion state of Colorado.

Benefits of the Personhood Battle in Colorado

Colorado Right to Life reached a place in 2006 that very closely paralleled our history in Georgia. Its prolife leadership repented of the direction in which they had been heading and turned the organization away from a natural law strategy and its attendant legal positivism. They sought the Lord and were led to support a Personhood amendment to their state constitution. Beginning in the summer of 2007, with little organization and virtually no money, they were able to collect 103,377 signatures from the people of Colorado, placing the amendment on the statewide ballot in 2008. They lost, with a mere 27% of the voters supporting the amendment.

To many prolife activists who accept a reductionist view of God's dealings in history, the outcome in Colorado has been criticized as imprudent, ill-timed, politically harmful, legally flawed—overall a disaster for the cause.

The same arguments were leveled against Georgia Right to Life when we challenged the conventional wisdom of the prolife movement by changing our endorsement criteria in 2000. Let's examine Colorado through the lens of long-term faithfulness to the biblical principle of Personhood.

First, I would argue, they succeeded; they succeeded in raising abortion as a continuing and relevant issue of debate, both locally in Colorado and nationally. Abortion had for a number of years been waning as a significant issue in the public eye. In 2002, Fox News conducted exit polling throughout a sampling of states. Abortion registered as an issue statistically relevant in state politics in only three states. As a result of changing to a Personhood message, the movement was energized with new money, new hope and new life. The debate was reframed for a new generation of voters. *TIME* magazine and *U.S. News and World Report* both published articles in 2007 about the efforts to pass Personhood in Colorado and Georgia.[141]

Second, it reduced the issue to a simple concept of human rights. "The idea is as simple as it is bold," reported Bret Schulte, legal correspondent for *U.S. News and World Report*.[142] This simple conclusion by Georgia House Representative Martin Scott "The taking of a life, no matter how old or how young, demands justice"[143] eloquently states our basic premise, "That Justice demands the legal protection of all innocent human life." This is accomplished whenever a government recognizes the Personhood of whatever human class is in question.

Personhood so simple a concept that even the very young can grasp its implications. Any seasoned political consultant will tell you that political ads need to be geared to a sixth-grade level of understanding. The public is very much like a sixth grader in terms of its attention span and comprehension of political issues. By distancing our dialogue from talk about court decisions and legal reasons for inaction, we force the abortion-minded public to consider the issue at a more basic level than feminist rights. The dialogue is in fact recalibrated to be about human rights. If we fail to make this connection, the abortion-minded public is confused as to why we prolifers are opposed to abortion in most cases but seemingly approve it based on the child's manner of conception (the rape or incest exceptions). The leaders of our prolife movement damage the simplicity of our message when they devalue any class of human life.

Battling Our Own National Prolife Leaders

It is especially troubling to see this trend move beyond the classic rape and incest debate. In perhaps one of the most troubling dialogues in recent history, Counsel for National Right to Life Committee James Bopp Jr., speaking before the 2008 National Republican Platform Committee on the subject of destructive human research, actually spoke in opposition to an amendment to the Republican platform that would have banned all deadly research at an embryonic level. He argued that the death of a child at an embryonic level was permissible as long as its "therapeutic" value was the objective.[144] Reporting on the incident in the *National Review Online*, reporter Stephen Spruiell observed that

> North Carolina delegate Mary Summa offered what appeared on the surface to be a small change. Summa sought to change the sentence: "We call for a ban on human cloning and a ban on the creation of **and** experimentation on human embryos for research purposes" to read "We call

for a ban on human cloning and a ban on the creation of **or** experimentation on human embryos for research purposes," thus severing experimentation on human embryos from their creation for that purpose. It's just one word, but it has huge implications. It is a call for a total ban on embryonic stem-cell research, including privately funded research using frozen embryos from in-vitro fertilization (IVF) clinics . . . .

In introducing her amendment, Summa gave an emotional speech in which she said, "I want my five children to live in a world where the weak are protected from the strong. I want them to live in a world where all life is protected."

The amendment drew opposition from Indiana delegate and prolife activist James Bopp Jr. . . . .

He added, "We should not be in the business of prohibiting therapeutic research. . . ."

Bopp then offered his own amendment to Summa's amendment. At this point Burr broke it up. He instructed Summa, Bopp and Kobach to confer until they had come up with a single amendment on stem-cells. The committee then moved on to other matters.

When the three of them returned, Summa's eyes were red and swollen. She re-submitted her original amendment, without modification. Burr called for a vote, and the motion passed.

The 2008 Republican Platform calls for a ban on all embryonic stem-cell research, public or private.[145]

It's a sad day when the Republican platform is more pro-Personhood than the legal counsel for the National Right to Life Committee. The situation approaches scandal when we recognize that no major prolife organization spoke out to censor Bopp's comments, which approve the destruction of a child at an embryonic level, as long as it furthers our scientific knowledge in pursuit of "therapeutic" advances. The Georgia Senate passed a ban on "therapeutic cloning" in its 2009 legislative session.[146] Many who spoke in opposition to the bill did so on the basis of the same reasoning put forward by Mr. Bopp. This is yet another example of a natural law worldview in opposition to a divine law position. Is it any wonder that the public is confused by our inconsistent stand for the sanctity of life? Imagine what the prolife movement could do if it spoke with a unified voice, using Personhood as our primary message and divine law as our roadmap?

Our Battle Against the Lord

I believe that we live in a day that has seen the gracious hand of God bless our nation. I also believe that my children and grandchildren may see that day end. My belief is grounded in my understanding of the immutable attribute of God's character known as Justice. Because he is the same yesterday, today and forever (Hebrews 13:8), there is a theological position held by many in the prolife movement that his attribute of Immutability (unchangeableness) and Justice (judgment of sin) is bearing down on our nation in some form of judgment—it is not a question of *if*, it is a question of *when*.

This sobering theme reoccurs throughout the history of God's people Israel. It is the assurance of God's long-suffering patience towards his wayward people followed by the promise of future judgment. Moses records this warning multiple times in the Old Testament. In Numbers 14:18 he declares, "The LORD is slow to anger and abounding in steadfast love, forgiving iniquity and transgression, but he will by no means clear the guilty, visiting the iniquity of the fathers on the children, to the third and the fourth generation." Our modern culture complains that this delay of judgment is unfair. It is the father's generation that sinned, but it is the children's generation that must pay. Sound familiar? Have you tallied out our national debt lately? This objection is not new. Jeremiah the prophet, after delivering a warning to the people of his day, had the same objection flung back into his face, "The fathers have eaten sour grapes, and the children's teeth are set on edge?" (Jer. 31:29). "How is this just?" you might ask. The answer is based in the character of God, specifically his attribute of Justice in which sin must be atoned. Unlike our personal credit or national debt, there is an eternal, immutable requirement in the holiness and justice of God that sin *must* be paid for *in full*. God's Justice demands atonement for sin at both the personal and national level.

Personal Atonement

From a personal perspective, Paul speaks of Christ's atonement in this respect, "for all have sinned and fall short of the glory of God, and are justified by his grace as a gift, through the redemption that is in Christ Jesus, whom God put forward as a propitiation by his blood, to be received by faith. This was to show God's righteousness, because in his divine forbearance he had passed over former sins. It was to show his righteousness at the present time, so that he might be just and the justifier of the one who has faith in Jesus." (Romans 3:23-26) Each one of us have sinned against God's righteous standard and require a blood sacrifice to atone for our sin. These verses simply mean that by the shedding of his innocent blood on the cross, Jesus bore the wrath of God against sin. This is procured and applied personally by having faith in Jesus. Once appropriated, this fully satisfies God's justice.

National Atonement for Bloodguiltiness

Can a nation be held accountable by God for its national sins? Historically we see evidence of this throughout the biblical narrative, and in particular for God's own people Israel. In 2 Chronicles 24:20 God spoke through a young man named Zechariah during a period of national apostasy, "Why do you break the commandments of the LORD, so that you cannot prosper? Because you have forsaken the LORD, he has forsaken you'". King Joash killed Zechariah for pointing out this truth and seeking to dissuade Israel from forsaking the divine law. Zechariah's murder exposed Israel nationally to the justice of God. King Joash had committed an especially heinous sin referred to as the shedding of "innocent blood"; otherwise known as "bloodguilt". [147] Other kings of Israel filled the land with the shedding of innocent blood, so much so, that this sin is listed as the actual reason for their annihilation as a nation for a period. "Surely this came upon Judah at the command of the Lord, to remove them out of his sight, for the sins of Manasseh, according to all that he had done, and also for the innocent blood that he had shed. For he filled Jerusalem with innocent blood, and the Lord would not pardon." (2 Kings 24:3,4). "The biblical concept of bloodguilt derives from the belief that deeds generate consequences and that sin, in particular, is a danger to the sinner. The most vivid examples of this belief appear in connection with unlawful homicide, where innocent blood (*dam naki* (*naqi*); Jonah 1:14) cries out for vengeance (Gen. 4:10), is rejected by the earth (Isa. 26:21; Ezek. 24:7), and pollutes it (Num. 35:33–34)."[148] A land, a nation-state can be polluted by the shedding of innocent blood. Certainly, the collective death of over 53 million children by abortion constitutes the sin of blood guiltiness.

God's justice demands atonement. How is the concept of atonement applied to a nation? It is clear that our founding fathers, and not a small number of former Presidents, believed that national calamity falls on our nation whenever we ignore God's divine law.

Founding father George Mason, prophetically proclaimed, "As nations can not be rewarded or punished in the next world they must be in this. By an inevitable chain of causes and effects, providence punishes national sins, by national calamities!"[149] And a short distance from our nation's Capitol, our third president Thomas

Jefferson has his words inscribed with an iron stylus on blocks of white marble, "And can the liberties of a nation be thought secure, when we have removed their only firm basis, a conviction in the minds of the people that these liberties are of the gift of God? That they are not to be violated but with his wrath? Indeed I tremble for my country when I reflect that God is just: that his justice can not sleep forever."

On March 30, 1863, in the midst of our great Civil War, President Abraham Lincoln placed the cause of war in a different context than his desire to emancipate the slaves. These words are recorded in his National Day of Prayer proclamation,

"It is the duty of nations as well as of men to own their dependence upon the overruling power of God; to confess their sins and transgressions in humble sorrow, yet with assured hope that genuine repentance will lead to mercy and pardon; and to recognize the sublime truth, announced in the Holy Scriptures and proven by all history, that those nations are blessed whose God is the Lord.

We know that by His divine law, nations, like individuals, are subjected to punishments and chastisements in this world. May we not justly fear that the awful calamity of civil war which now desolates the land may be a punishment inflicted upon us for our presumptuous sins, to the needful end of our national reformation as a whole people?

We have been the recipients of the choicest bounties of heaven; we have been preserved these many years in peace and prosperity; we have grown in numbers, wealth and power as no other nation has ever grown. *But we have forgotten God.* We have forgotten the gracious hand which preserved us in peace and multiplied and enriched and strengthened us, and we have vainly imagined, in the deceitfulness of our hearts, that all these blessings were produced by some superior wisdom and virtue of our own. Intoxicated with unbroken success, we have become too self-sufficient to feel the necessity of redeeming and preserving grace, too proud to pray to the God that made us.

It behooves us then, to humble ourselves before the offended Power, to confess our national sins, and to pray for clemency and forgiveness . . . no less than the pardon of our national sins . . . ."

Summary

As former state Director for David Bryant's, Concerts of Prayer, I have personally led citywide prayer meetings that confessed our sins and implored God's mercy on us and our children for the "sins of our fathers". My personal experience of corporate prayer has led me to believe that the clock of God's judgment, for us as a nation, is quickly counting down. Because God *is* slow to anger and abounding in steadfast love, forgiving iniquity and transgression, we have the assurance that our National Day of Prayer, organizations such as 40 Days for Life, Bound for Life, and other prayer focused ministries and their continued public confession has perhaps delayed his judgment in our current generation. I believe that it is possible that the next generation can experience the same delay. But ultimately, I believe that God in his Justice must call our nation to account for not only the 53+ million children killed by abortion, but the elderly who are being cast onto the refuge pile of spent humanity, the disabled who are being labeled "non-persons" and those at an embryonic level that may never experience the same level of humanness that we enjoy. At some point our national prayer of "God bless America" can no longer expect to be answered. From the perspective of atonement, I pray that we never hear these words at a national level, "you shall not be cleansed anymore till I have satisfied my fury upon you" (Ezekiel 24:13).

Chapter 9

Personhood:
What Is at Stake If We Fail?

In the 20ᵗʰ century it was enough that we were prolife, but in the 21ˢᵗ century we must also be pro-human.

Nigel Cameron,
Former dean of the Wilberforce Forum

Whether we worship it in the marketplace for its ability to create wealth or as the purest expression of human endeavor, science is a god of unintended consequences.

Robert Lee Hotz,
Science writer for *The Los Angeles Times*

Please note that the following short story is a work of fiction based upon current biotech policy and actual scientific achievements. Please avail yourself of the endnotes to properly evaluate the risks, challenges, and fears of a post-human future. My sole purpose is to make you aware that the public policy of the future is being decided today . . . we as a movement are largely silent. Should we be concerned? I not only believe we should, I believe it is imperative if we are to remain "salt and light" to a culture. which has lost its moral bearings.

(A.D. 2101)

It was the dawn of a new day, as well as of a new age.

Just moments from cresting the small mountain ridge to the east, the hidden glory of the sun's radiance painted a pink lining on the quickly dispersing storm clouds. It was the "time between times"— the diffuse light of morning just prior to sunrise. The pink sapphire sky held the promise of a colorful June morning in the foothills of north Georgia's ancient Appalachian mountain chain.

Mountain mists rose in gossamer threads toward the crests of the low-lying hills. With an ethereal twist of motion and muted light, these mountain spirits, formed from the womb of an early morning thunderstorm, spiraled upward from the mountain coves toward the eternal heavens.

This was the moment that Sam savored each morning. Renowned cybernetic biokinesisist and daily psi-commuter to Atlanta's Center for Disease Control (CDC), Dr. Samuel Bates looked forward each morning to that exact moment the sun breached Amicolola Ridge.

His routine was unerring. Rain or shine and invariably dressed for the season, Sam moved outdoors to his protected roost. He greeted each new dawn by setting his oversized, handmade clay mug on the rich brown cypress table that was the centerpiece of his elevated outdoor deck. Filled to the brim with rich, dark coffee, his own mountain sprite rose delicately from the steaming mug and joined the ghostly band of heaven-bound spirits.

His home-office, adjoined with his remote laboratory, was nestled against the backdrop of a lush pine forest perched high atop a lonely mountain cove. With no neighbors in view, this former national forest retreat provided Sam with the privacy his work demanded and his life craved. The advent of the hydrogen fuel cell and the limitless power provided by a water-fueled engine[150] together allowed private residences to become islands far removed from the market providers.

Sam's personal and professional needs were supplied daily to his home port via drone delivery.

The aroma of fresh-made coffee completed the sensory experience Sam expected each morning as he gazed at the colorful mountain panorama that unfolded from his elevated perch. Sam personally believed that this self-imposed ritual was necessary to provide a "baseline" for his natural sensory powers before allowing his psi-companion, Eshah, to come online and augment his human perception with a blizzard of extrasensory data. He relished this last bastion of privacy before opening himself up to the unending stream of data that would assault him the moment he logged in to his psi-connection.[151]

The fury of last night's storm had dissipated, and the sky heralded a red dawn. *"Red sky at morning, sailors take warning,"* mused Dr. Sam Bates as he gazed out at the moisture-laden mountain laurel. The morning wind blew upon the spindly sassafras tree, causing it to drop brilliant pearls of color from its many three-fingered mitts. Sam would never have accepted the fact, but this also portended an appropriate prophetic warning for a culture that prided itself in being not only post-Christian but also post-human. *Carpe Diem.* The age was about to be seized by the day.

As the morning sun burned through the storm-induced haze, it created a diffuse world of hidden objects. The wraithlike images of mountain trolls encased in fog quickly transformed into lightning-scarred hickory and red oak, which were suddenly revealed in brilliant flashes of clarity, color, and detail; and then just as quickly they returned to patches of otherworldly vision obscured in the mist. Like a toy kaleidoscope in the unyielding grip of an awestruck toddler, the line between fantasy and reality blurred, creating a naturally occurring psychedelic experience.

Ironic, mused Sam as he looked expectantly toward the delivery zone. *This is one of those rare occasions when Nature mimics human technology.* The Neural Net, a blending of human perception and computer enhancement, produced a mental state that had moved the human race to transcend the limits of its physical senses. It had granted humans the ability to focus their minds with laser-like precision on whatever object or query they wished to illuminate. Simply conceive the thought, and the Neural Net shone the light of knowledge on the subject, thereby dispelling the fog of ignorance.

What insight, lucidity, and power it gives to one who possesses access to the Net. It's a pity so few can enjoy this transcendence, thought Sam. *But then human government in the 22nd century doesn't require the input of the masses but merely the informed oversight of a very representative technocrati.* Long ago, on the altars of science and convenience, the masses had quietly traded their individual freedoms for the security of being ruled by an informed, benevolent technological oligarchy.

Sam was a member of that anointed class, set apart from the masses and from other emerging sentient life. One could almost describe his calling and vocation as "holy." Sam felt his duties and responsibilities toward the "have nots" quite keenly. Science was the prevailing religion of the 22nd century, and Sam, as a scientist of international renown, was one of its high priests.

The Neural Net, as Sam was well aware, was the grandchild of the former U.S. military defense agency, DARPA,[152] and its early 21st-century machine project the Deep Learning program.[153] Tasked with harnessing exponential increases in computer processing power, its goal was to emulate human perception by means of self-learning algorithms. The Deep Learning program had produced striking results, most importantly it had been the immediate forerunner to the Singularity.[154]

Prophesied to arrive in the 2040's, the Singularity had burst upon the scene a full decade sooner than anyone had expected. By definition, the Singularity was that eagerly anticipated time in human history when artificial intelligence attained the same level of processing power as the human brain, thereby replicating the power of human thought—albeit void of self-consciousness and personality. It would be another two decades before that processing power reached the Turin stage[155]—the stage at which artificial intelligence and human personality would become indistinguishable to casual, third-party observers.

In the 2060's computers possessed self-awareness, sentience, and personality—on this basis proclaiming themselves to be "human." They, as a sentient class, had demanded Personhood under the law. AIs (artificial intelligences) had been granted that recognition by a Supreme Court ruling that extended the right of Personhood found in the 28th Amendment to the U.S. Constitution, otherwise known as the Personhood Amendment. The passage of the Personhood Amendment in 2024 had established that all *human* life had an inalienable right to life, a right that must be protected from a *human*'s earliest biological beginning and extend through natural death. This stunning legislative victory had marked the end of half a century of prolife efforts. Having achieved its singular objective, the legal recognition of Personhood, the prolife movement had quietly and quickly dissipated.

By 2080, through the advances made in the biomedical field of nanotechnology,[156] the biometric interface was developed. By definition this was a subdural wireless brain implant whose transmitter enabled, for the first time, full human-machine interface and the exponential expansion of consciousness and knowledge that it accessed. Powered by human metabolism, the interface required extra calories to be consumed by the host in order to prevent the occurrence of weight loss. Indeed, since the majority of hosts did not significantly increase their calorific intake, most enjoyed an ideal weight. Many of the diseases that had plagued the overweight citizens of the 20th century had been virtually eradicated by the low body fat engendered by increased metabolic functions.

Transhumanism, a biological Big Bang, had exploded into

existence, creating a new era in which humankind no longer believed people were "created in the image of God." Instead, humans became the creator of a new being, "homo perfectus"[157] (H+),[158] a being "created in the image of Man." By picking up where evolution left off, post-humanity realized the long-cherished dream of being "like God." Birthed in the last decade of the 21st century, the Transhumanist era grew from its infancy in the 2010's to adolescence in the first decade of the 22nd century—a dangerous time in the life cycle of any creature.

The Cybernetic Artificial Intelligence Network (CAIN) was a predictable offshoot of the biometric interface. Sam ought to know; he had fathered the first CAIN construct and even today was enjoying the companionship of Eshah, his most advanced creation. Named for the wife of the biblical Cain,[159] Eshah was NOT an "artificial" intelligence. She was sentient and self-aware, legally imbued with Personhood and able to provide an almost infinite stream of data, extrasensory perception, and personal companionship. By means of the biometric interface, a CAIN construct could directly interface with the entire human neural system, including the pleasure centers of the human brain. CAIN was to a 22nd century adult what the personal computer had been to a 20th century Internet surfer, albeit with an exponential expansion of the term "personal."

Each of the sensory regions of the brain could be manipulated to emulate and enhance all five of the senses: Taste and touch, sight and sound combined with the olfactory functions to create a sensory experience without boundaries. One could travel to a foreign land and explore the exotic sights and smells of a seaside villa or enjoy an evening of fine food and music without ever having to leave the confines of home.

A simulated experience was an enhanced experience, in every way superior to simple human perceptions. In a sim environment, Corelli's Christmas Concerto was not just an auditory experience, but a spiritual high. Combined with a full array of sensory accompaniments, it immersed the recipient in a universe of sight and sound, taste and smell that transcended the merely heavenly and approached the beatific. Because such a heightened sense of pleasure had been found to be psychologically addictive, the size of the Pleasure Bandwidth was strictly regulated and restricted by the U.N. Regulatory Commission on Mental Health.

Eshah, did last week's riots in Paris and Rio de Janeiro persuade the Commission to expand the Pleasure Bandwidth? inquired Sam as he broke from his private reverie and engaged his psi-companion for the first time that day.

He posted the query through his conversational filter. Years ago scientists had learned that the conceptual flow of thought was hardcoded in human speech. Language couldn't be replaced by a flood of omniscient data streams, so the biometric filters had been developed to simulate human conversation.

Good morning, Sam. I've missed you. You know that the hours you sleep or are offline are an eternity to me!

Eshah, you need to get yourself another boyfriend or two . . . . in Australia, if that's the way you feel, teased Sam.

Actually, I have the capacity to fully interact with over a million human sessions . . . concurrently . . . but you know that, don't you, Sam? comm'ed Eshah, adding the perception of a slightly protruding nonexistent lower lip.

Aahh, but that's precisely why I selfishly keep you to myself, Eshah. Who wants to be constantly compared to a million other partners? responded Sam, employing the mental equivalent of a "smiley face."

Back to your question . . . It appears to be the consensus among the technocrati that the U.N. will make some form of nominal concession and allow an increase of "soma" in the domain of general well-being. It isn't likely to permit any wholesale increase to the direct pleasure stimulators, reported Eshah.

Eshah was omnipresent. Residing on the Neural Net, but present wherever Sam went, Eshah was the only daily companion in Sam's sheltered existence. "She" being the first CAIN construct, he intended to keep it that way while she remained in the beta stage. Other constructs existed, but none could boast the level of development Eshah demonstrated whenever they were tested side-by-side with her. Eshah's Turin scores were off the charts.

Sam had one other companion, his collaborative partner at the CDC, Dr. Henry Wright. Henry was the only other human for whom Sam had any personal feeling. His respect and admiration for Henry, in fact, knew no limits. Henry had mentored Sam as a graduate student of Cybernetic Biokinesis and had been instrumental in prodding him toward the monumental task of developing the CAIN construct. His encouragement, technocratic alliances, and sponsorship had, without doubt, enabled Sam to become the leading authority in the field.

Aldrous Huxley had it wrong: There is no danger of falling prey to unlimited "soma" exposure in the post-human age. The Commission has a handle on the situation; now if law enforcement could just succeed in closing down the clandestine unlimited bandwidth parlors that are agitating the masses . . .

Similar to the illegal opium dens of the 18th century, Unlimited Pleasure Palaces (UPPs) operated clandestinely, but were quickly detected because of their massive bandwidth requirements. For every UPP that law enforcement shut down, three more would spring into existence, giving their patrons anything and everything they desired.

Hedonists have existed in every age, Sam thought aloud, *and their numbers are self-limiting. Like a moth to flame, they burn out in the heat of unending sensual pleasure. Which is a good thing, as we would soon see the collapse of society and civilization if hedonism were allowed to proliferate unchecked. My faith and trust are in the U.N.'s ability to adroitly regulate the masses. Surely last week's riots were a societal anomaly.*

Speaking of regulation, Sam, your request for sexual/asexual reproduction (SAR) has been granted by the Commission for Human Propagation. Congratulations, Sam. I'm very happy for you and Henry.[160] *You'll want to schedule the cellular donation ceremony as soon as possible. Who should we invite to witness the consummation of your donation?*

SAR[161] had developed over the past century. From its experimental beginnings in 2012, it had taken only a few years to precipitate a total revolution in childbearing and redefinition of the family. Male sperm and female eggs were produced from nasal skin cells from one or two persons of either human gender by reprogramming the cells to revert to a stem cell stage. They were then combined in vitro for fertilization to take place. Indeed, a single individual could provide both egg and sperm, thus cloning themselves and producing a child in their own image.

With the perfecting of the ectogenic womb in 2018, women were no longer needed for their reproductive services.[162] Freed of these reproductive shackles, abortion and the right to privacy became moot points. A woman who found herself in an unwanted pregnancy could, through a medical procedure that was less invasive than abortion, remove the tiny developing child and transfer it to an artificial womb, where it became a ward of the state until viability, Post viability it was placed into one of the many adoptive homes. Adoptive homes were easy to find—waiting lists had mushroomed as more and more same sex couples demanded to enter the ranks of parenthood.

Women, for the first time in history, were actually competing on a level playing surface with men. The nurturing societal influence of Motherhood had been replaced by something sterile and empty. Society as a whole suffered a temporary setback as mothering gave place to mentoring, and the secure environment of a mother's womb gave way to vats and super-oxygenated fluids in vitro.

Eshah, that's wonderful news. Thanks. Let me give it some thought. By the way, Eshah, I ordered the ecto-womb several weeks ago. Can you give me an update on its arrival data?

It's scheduled to arrive at our delivery port by land drone at 2:45 p.m. today, responded Eshah. *It has been noted on your itinerary for several days now,* Eshah chided. *I requested two sim-kids to accompany the delivery. The total weight is over 200 kilos.*

"Sim-kids" or "humanzees,"[163] as they had once been known, were the result of careful genetic enhancements introduced into a strain of simian-human hybrids developed by Emory University in the middle of the last century. Initially classed by society as a repulsive scientific exercise, their benefits as a source of cheap labor (not to mention DARPA's military applications)[164] had quickly overcome the public's aversion to this parody of human existence. Childlike in their mental capabilities and yet strong and agile in limb and leg, sim-kids were implanted with a biometric interface that regulated aggression and discouraged violent displays by means of manipulating pain sensors. While generally reliable, this form of control was not 100% certain and a new means of control was needed. Henry's work at the CDC was close to releasing a revolutionary new means of assuring complete submission and subservience in simkids.

Able to master human language via the aid of their interface, they had become the ideal answer to menial labor needs. This semi-human class of brute laborer was literally fed peanuts and paid for its services by an infusion of somatic stimulation of its members' rudimentary pleasure centers. Humankind had solved the class labor struggle by freeing itself of all menial tasks and petty toil. True, a fringe element of society clamored for Personhood for the sim-kids, but their utility and convenience assured that the public would never vote to allow them this right. Like the prolife movement of the previous century, GRASP[165] was committed to educating the general public until a shift in public opinion forced the regulators to deal with the emancipation of this human-hybrid race and to grant Personhood to this oppressed and abused class of beings. If the artificial intelligence agents had succeeded in gaining Personhood, then surely it would br only a matter of time before sim-kids would come to enjoy this freedom from the bottom of their spiritless beings.

Sam was about to respond to Eshah's query when his personal communications interface activated. This particular interface emoted the highest sense of urgency and flooded Sam with a sense of dread. Only one individual had this level of clearance—Henry!

Sam!

Henry, what's wrong, I . . .

Listen Sam, you have to act now and do exactly as I say. I don't know how much time I have. There's been a construction breach at the CDC, and we have a Level 4 shutdown. I'm afraid that our synthetic life form has been loosed in the wild. Sam, the sim-kid hosts are loose—do you hear me? You must activate your Level 4 protocol . . . NOW! There are whole neighborhoods around Emory reporting areas of infection. There's a quantifiable lack of psi-activity from Atlanta's affected areas. It's only a matter of wind speed and direction before north Georgia is affected.

Momentarily stunned, Sam recovered his presence of mind and immediately instructed Eshah to launch the Level 4 protocols, *and cancel the delivery. Quarantine all outside exposures and give me an inventory of food and professional supplies.*

Which synthetic life form was it, Henry? What are we dealing with? Please don't tell me it's the Synthia Strain.

First developed by the J. Craig Venter Institute in 2010,[166] Synthia beta 1.0 claimed the distinction of being the world's first synthetic life form. Based on the earlier Human Genome Project, genetic science had greatly enhanced humanity's understanding of biological life by means of digitizing biology through the conversion of DNA's four basic building blocks, G, A, T, and C, into the computer language of 1's and 0's. This had led to computers being used to design life forms, like Synthia, not found in nature.

In 2055 post-Singularity software had actually begun producing the prophesied hope of the 2010 Millennium Project: "Synthetic biologists forecast [that] as computer code is written to create life forms to augment human capabilities, so too genetic code will be written to create life forms that will augment civilization."[167] The natural progression of digital biology produced better dogs, cats, horses, and cows. It also produced a better mouse, which of course, necessitated an exponentially better mousetrap. This was also the origin of sim-kids and the promise of augmenting human labor with a specialized sub-class of human-animal hybrids.

Sam, I have just sent you my most current lab notes on Synthia 9.8. We were very close to closing the biohazard gate between sim-kids and humans. I'm afraid our conclusions have shown that the final modifications must be applied to the human genome through germline intervention.[168] We just have to change the human genome to remove the peptide bridge that Synthia 9.8 uses to infect humans. That done, our goal of fully sentient sim-kids, with no concern for personal aspirations, will be complete . . . an unending supply of biological servants with no disease, aging, or rebellious tendencies of aspiring to human status . . . a creature void of volition and posing no risk to humanity.

Rushing inside, Sam's fears morphed the dawning of this day into a full, waking nightmare. He knew from his close collaboration with Henry that Henry had succeeded in producing the desired effect in sim-kids via Synthia 9.8. Precisely how the life form removed personal volition without impairing sentience was still being investigated—thus the sim-kid trials at the Primate Center at Emory. Also clearly established was that a "firewall" had to be established on the human side of the equation because Synthia 9.8 could produce the same effect in humans. The PNA project was in its final stages of completion.[169]

How ironic, thought Sam ruefully with his privacy filter engaged,

Here's a bug from which Eshah is fully protected.

True, Eshah was susceptible to computer-generated viruses, but never anything so sinister that a good backup couldn't cure. Humanity had long ago acknowledged its desire for a post-human construct.

If the PNA changes were introduced as the cure for Synthia 9.8, perhaps now would be a good time to "back up" the human race.

Henry, how did this happen? asked Sam, dismayed.

A new set of labs was being constructed deep in the granite bedrock across the street from the Primate Center; new lab space was needed for the final stage of testing. A chunk of granite the size of basketball must have escaped the blast net,[170] *sending a ballistic missile through the Level 4 cages of the Primate Center. Sam, the simkids are loose!*[171] *There's no effective barrier for stopping this infection. Sam . . . I . . .*

Henry . . . say again?

I . . . I . . . feel so . . . I'm going to sit right . . . I'm tired. I need to sleep.

Henry, what's wrong? Eshah, enhance the connection. Give me all the available data Henry is streaming.

Sam, Henry's sight data is offline, but his vitals and hearing are normal. I detect sim-kid conversations in the background.

Summary

My goal in this last chapter was to expose the prolife activist to the emerging world of the new biotech century. I have purposely projected an ultimate Personhood victory for all human life, born or preborn. I have also projected the end of the prolife movement because it is, at its heart, anti-abortion as opposed to pro-sanctity of human life.

As you check out the endnotes for this chapter, you'll notice that this is not science fiction but a compendium of current events or events that we can certainly project into our near future. Policy is being debated today, and it is largely being decided without the voice of the grassroots activists who have been so successful in moving public opinion to oppose abortion.

If we are to avoid this post-human future, we must expand our sanctity-of-life focus to embrace a biblical worldview and then disseminate our message to the general public without appearing to come across in the process as anti-technology Luddites. This will be our challenge in the 21st century. I pray we will be successful.

Prolife Passages in the Bible

God Is the Creator of Life

Genesis 1:27, 2:7	Job 12:10	Psalm 139:13-16
1 Samuel 2:6	Job 31:15	Isaiah 64:8
Nehemiah 9:6	Job 33:4	Acts 17:24-25
Job 10:8-12	Psalm 100:3	Colossians 1:16

Children Are a Gift from God

Genesis 18:10-14	Genesis 48:9	Proverbs 17:6
Genesis 25:21	1 Samuel 1:19-20	Isaiah 8:18
Genesis 29:31-35	Psalm 113:9	Hosea 9:11
Genesis 30:1-2, 22-23	Psalm 127:3-5	
Genesis 33:5	Psalm 128:3	

Personhood Begins at Conception

Job 10:8-12	Jeremiah 20:17a	Luke 1:35-38
Psalm 51:5	Matthew 1:18-20	

Personhood Exists in the Womb

Genesis 16:11a	Psalm 71:5-6	Isaiah 49:1, 5a
Genesis 25:22-24	Psalm 139:13-16	Jeremiah 1:5
Job 3:11, 16	Ecclesiastes 5:15a	Hosea 12:3a
Job 31:15	Isaiah 7:14	Luke 1:13-15
Psalm 22:9-10	Isaiah 44:2, 24	Luke 1:39-44
Psalm 58:3, 8b	Isaiah 46:3	Galatians 1:15a

God Determines the Length of Life

1 Samuel 2:6a   Job 14:5   Psalm 139:16

God's View of Abortion

Exodus 20:13   Deuteronomy 30:19   Matthew 19:18b
Exodus 23:7   Proverbs 6:16-19   Romans 13:9a, 10a

Christ's Esteem of Children

Isaiah 40:11   Matthew 18:2-4, 10, 14   Mark 10:13-14
Matthew 10:42   Mark 9:37

Parents' Love for Children

Genesis 21:16   2 Samuel 12:16   Mark 5:23
Genesis 31:28   2 Samuel 21:8-10   Luke 15:20
Genesis 37:35   1 Kings 3:26   John 16:21-22
Exodus 2:3   2 Kings 4:20   John 19:25
1 Samuel 2:19   Matthew 15:22

Sacrifice of Children Forbidden

Exodus 1:15-17   Deuteronomy 18:10a, 12   Psalm 106:31-38
Leviticus 18:21, 24, 30   2 Kings 16:3   Jeremiah 32:35
Leviticus 20:1-5   2 Kings 17:17   Ezekiel 16:20-21
Deuteronomy 12:31   2 Kings 21:6

Punishment for Causing an Abortion

Exodus 21:22-25   Proverbs 28:17a   Amos 1:13
Deuteronomy 27:25a

Protecting the Fatherless Is Our Responsibility

Isaiah 1:23   Zechariah 7:9-10   James 1:27
Isaiah 10:1-2   Matthew 19:14

Fetal Abnormalities of Birth Defects and Abortion

Exodus 4:11	Psalm 94:9	Romans 8:28
Exodus 20:13	Isaiah 45:9-12a	Romans 9:20-21
Leviticus 19:14	John 9:1-3	1 Corinthians 1:27

Mother's Mental Health and Abortion

Exodus 20:13	Matthew 15:19	Ephesians 4:18
1 Kings 3:26-27	Romans 1:26-28	

Rape or Incest and Abortion

Genesis 19:36-38	Deuteronomy 24:16	Romans 8:28
Genesis 38:13-26	Ruth 4:18-22	Ephesians 5:20
Genesis 50:20	Matthew 1:3	
Exodus 20:13	Luke 3:33	

Sexual Immorality and Abortion

Genesis 16:2, 4a, 15	Genesis 38	Micah 6:7b-8
Genesis 21:10-13	Ruth 4:12	

Imitating the World Is Forbidden

Genesis 9:7	Proverbs 1:10-19	Romans 8:5, 7
Leviticus 18:21, 24, 29-30	Proverbs 15:3	Romans 12:2
Numbers 35:33	Isaiah 5:20-21, 23	Colossians 2:8
Psalm 10:5-11	Isaiah 59:7	2 Peter 2:2-3
Psalm 94:21	Lamentations 4:3, 6, 10	

Our Accountability to God

Genesis 9:1, 5-6	Jeremiah 7:5-6	Galatians 6:10

Silence Is Inexcusable

Esther 4:14-16	Isaiah 1:10-17	Matthew 9:36-38
Job 31:14-15	Ezekiel 3:16-19	Matthew 18:14
Proverbs 24:11-12	Hosea 4:6a	Ephesians 2:10
Proverbs 29:10	Matthew 5:16	

Our Responsibility

Deuteronomy 30:19	Ezekiel 3:16-19	1 John 3:18

Empirical Data: A Decade of Pragmatic Political Gain for GRTL

2000

- On July 17, 2000, GRTL's board disqualified any and all legislators and candidates seeking office if they held a "prolife" position that permitted abortions for cases of rape and incest.
- Our legislature had none of the NRLC-recommended prolife legislation except for two deeply flawed statutes: Partial Birth Ban and Parental Notification.
- 3% of our legislature held to "no exceptions" stances.

2001

- Within a year *every* member of the newly elected GOP State Executive Board held to a "*no exceptions*" (NE) position, advocating that abortion should be illegal except in cases where the mother's life is in danger *and* only then after both the mother and child are treated equally in attempting to preserve life.
- Ralph Reed was elected chairman of the party.
- $400K was raised for our media campaign. Calls to pregnancy resource centers skyrocketed during the following year.

2002

- First election cycle with new NE criteria. 75% of endorsed races won.
- Gained 6 Senate seats (first ever prolife majority) and 18 House seats (NE).

- First prolife governor since Roe v. Wade was elected.
- Governor Sonny Perdue (NE) drew a record 5.6% of *all* Georgia voters *because* of his prolife stance (per Fox News exit polling). He won by a margin of only 5.2%.
- Exit polls showed that Georgia was one of only a few states in the nation that succeeded in raising the *abortion* issue to a statistically significant status among voters (9%).

2003

- Abortions increased .7% year on the year.
- Number of local GRTL chapters rose from 12-43.
- Money raised in 2002 was spent to purchase media targeting women in crisis pregnancy and increase public presence. TV ads aired for nine months of the year.

2004

- Abortions dropped 5.3% in 12 months after a full-year media campaign (3 weeks on and 1 week off).
- The Prolife Caucus in the Georgia House soared from 76 to 99 (91 needed to pass laws), up 23% over the elections in 2000. First-time majority in both houses.
- 75% of all GRTL PAC-endorsed candidates won.

2005

- Abortions dropped another 3 percent.
- Woman's Right to Know law passed after 15 years in the works. It included:
    - 24-hour waiting
    - Informed consent
    - Fetal pain
    - Removed loophole in Parental Notification law

- Americans United for Life prolife state ranking placed Georgia 22nd in the nation.

2006

- Abortions dropped 10.9%.
- Georgia only state in the nation that didn't lose *any* Republican seats during election cycle.
- Re-elected Governor Sonny Perdue and added first prolife lieutenant governor (NE).
- Added 5 in Georgia House (NE).
- 84% of GRTL PAC races won (100 of 119)!
- Passed prolife legislation.
  - Unborn Victims of Violence
  - Chose life tags
- Americans United for Life prolife state ranking rose to 20th in the nation.

2007

- Over the previous decade abortions fell 5.1% percent, while population of state increased 17.5%.
- Passed prolife legislation.
  - Woman's Ultrasound
  - Save the Cure (Adult Stem cell /Cord blood)
- Introduced the nation's first Personhood amendment at a state level.
- Americans United for Life prolife state ranking rose to 14th in the nation.

2008

- Didn't lose a single seat in the Georgia Senate and gained 1 in the Georgia House.

- 90% of GRTL PAC races won! This is up from 84% in 2006 and 75% in 2004.
- Pushed for passage of Personhood amendment—most co-signed piece of legislation in the 2008 session.
- Promoted the nation's first viable "No Exceptions" presidential candidate. Huckabee won Georgia.
- Only 11% of Evangelicals voted for Obama (third lowest in the nation).
- Americans United for Life prolife state ranking rose to 13th in the nation.

2009

- H.R. 5 (Human Life Amendment) filed in House.
- President pro tem of the Senate helped pass Advanced Reproductive Technology (S.B 169) bill in the Senate.
- Embryo Adoption Act which included legally defined Personhood is sponsored in House. Passed House and Senate to become the nation's first (HB 388).
- Americans United for Life prolife state ranking rose to 11th in the nation.

2010

- Filed and passed in the Senate (SB 529) a ban on gender-based abortion, race-based abortion, and all coerced abortion. Included wrongful death and private right of action. Passed all House committee hearings before being killed by the House Speaker on the last day of session.
- 92% of all GRTL-endorsed candidates won.
- Defeated Sarah Palin's "prolife" gubernatorial candidate with rape and incest exceptions in the primary.

- Passed the Personhood Amendment in a nonbinding vote during the July primary. All 46 counties affirmed the amendment—Republicans by a vote of 75% "Yes" and Democrats by a vote of 72% "Yes."
- All 9 statewide constitutional offices are now held by officials who have no exceptions and support a Personhood amendment to the Georgia constitution.
- African American "Endangered Species" campaign featured on front cover of June issue of *Focus Citizen Magazine.*
- Americans United for Life prolife state ranking rose to 8th in the nation.

Most prolife and/or pro-family organizations claim that they oppose Personhood because it doesn't work, arguing that it is neither politically prudent nor pragmatic. Georgia Right to Life has ten years of empirical data asserting the opposite, and we are not an anomaly. Colorado, Mississippi, and Florida are in the early stages of Personhood and have *not* enjoyed the support of the premier right-to-life organizations in their states, as we have in Georgia. Yet they are beginning to show similar results. The problem is not with the strategy of Personhood but with the lack of unity among prolife leaders. I remind the reader of the words of G. K. Chesterton: "Christianity has not been tried and found wanting; it has been found difficult and not tried." We have tried the biblical standard of Personhood and found it difficult, yet through perseverance and God's abundant grace we have found it to be highly prudent and pragmatic. *Sola Deo Gloria.*

Appendix 3

Online Personhood Resources

Governor Mike Huckabee on Personhood
www.youtube.com/watch?v=_8LNZtP35KA

www.Personhood.net

Sponsored by Georgia Right to Life, this is a central clearinghouse of information regarding Personhood. It contains public policy discussions and white papers on the leading biotech issues of the day. Originally intended for a local Georgia audience, it has gone international in its impact. See:

- Advocates of Personhood
- Policy, Strategy and Law Discussions
- Holocaust Memorial Wall (Virtual)

www.PersonhoodUSA.com

This is the premier U.S. site coordinating and reporting on the various state efforts to promote Personhood. Personhood USA desires to glorify Jesus Christ in a way that creates a culture of life, so that all innocent human lives may be protected by love and by law. Personhood USA serves the prolife community by assisting local groups to initiate citizen, legislative, and political action, focusing on the ultimate goal of the prolife movement: Personhood rights for all innocent humans.

personhoodeducation.org

Legal, medical, and strategic resources to aid the Personhood effort.

www.ALL.org

Has posted over 799 articles mentioning Personhood. American Life League is a 501(c)(3) organization cofounded in 1979 by Judie Brown. It is the largest grassroots Catholic prolife organization in the United States and is committed to the protection of all innocent human beings from the moment of creation to natural death. A.L.L. is a longtime promoter of Personhood.

- *Human Personhood and Ill-advised Catholic Bishops*
  www.renewamerica.com/columns/brown/091210
- Forsythe's Dilemma: Legal Positivism
  www.all.org/newsroom_judieblog.php?id=2781

www.thomasmore.org

The Thomas More Law Center is a not-for-profit public interest law firm dedicated to the defense and promotion of the religious freedom of Christians, time-honored family values, and the sanctity of human life. It supports a strong national defense and an independent and sovereign United States of America. In its site search function one can query "personhood" and find 40 informative articles promoting Personhood.

www.grtl.org/docs/ILM_Spring%2010.pdf
  Unborn Children as Constitutional Persons by Gregory J. Roden, J.D.

"Mr. Roden argues that the text of the Equal Protection Clause of the Fourteenth Amendment compels federal protection of unborn children as persons. Furthermore, he shows that to the extent the Court examined the substantive law in these disciplines, its legal conclusions were not warranted."[173]

James Bopp, Jr., J.D.
Editor-in-Chief
Issues in Law & Medicine, Spring 2010

Endnotes

1   Toronto Blue Jays, Canada.

2   Federal Communications Commission, n.d., http://www.fcc.gov/ogc/documents/opinions/1996/becker.html (accessed 1 March 2010).

3   Ibid. The case was remanded upon appeal to the United States Court of Appeals for the District Of Columbia Circuit, which ruled three years after the fact in my favor and fined the FCC over $100,000.00.

4   This is only an estimate that was given to me by CNN. The ad actually reached far more because it ran repeatedly for two days on all of the major news channels.

5   Georgia's Governor Nathan Deal

6   I define "*no*-exception" to mean that abortion should be illegal except in cases where the mother's life is in danger *and only* after both mother and child have been treated equally when attempting to preserve life.

7   Public Service Commissioner Tim Echols

8   The press references politicians who have earned our endorsement as having a "life of the mother" exception. We do not challenge this publicly. Our stated position is that we require all candidates to agree to our position: "GRTL opposes abortion at any point of gestation, as it destroys a living, growing human life. In the rare case that the mother's life is indeed endangered by a continuation of the pregnancy, sound medical practice would dictate that every effort be made to save both lives."

9   *Defending Life 2010: Proven Strategies for a Prolife America* (Washington, D.C.: Americans United for Life, 2010). p. 509.

10 Ronald Bailey, "The Pursuit of Happiness, Peter Singer interviewed by Ronald Bailey," http://reason.com/archives/2000/12/01/the-pursuit-of-happiness-peter , 2000, 1 (accessed 13 November 2010): "Singer's mother suffers from severe Alzheimer's disease, and so she no longer qualifies as a person by his own standards, yet he spends considerable sums on her care. This apparent contradiction of his principles has not gone unnoticed by the media. When I asked him about it during our interview at his Manhattan

apartment in late July, he sighed and explained that he is not the only person who is involved in making decisions about his mother (he has a sister). He did say that if he were solely responsible, his mother might not be alive today."

11   Ibid.

12   Peter Singer, "FAQs", n.d., http://www.princeton.edu/~psinger/faq.html (accessed 13 November 2010).

13   Andrew Pollack, "Engineering by Scientists on Embryo Stirs Criticism," *New York Times* (13 May 2008), http://www.nytimes.com/2008/05/13/science/13embryo.html (accessed 13 November 2010).

14   A short list includes 40 Days for Life founder David Bereit; Lila Rose, president of Live Action Films; and PersonhoodUSA founders Keith Mason and Cal Zastrow.

15   Joni Erikson Tada, Georgia Right to Life Personhood Symposium, 2008, http://www.personhoodPersonhood.net/index.php?option=com_wrapper&view=wrapper&Itemid=606 (accessed 13 November 2010).

16   We did have a Partial Birth Abortion Ban that was neutered and rendered useless by the Georgia Supreme Court.

17   It was offered in 46 counties on the Republican primary ballot of July 2010. In all 46 counties where the amendment was presented, it passed overwhelmingly by an amazing 75%! In the one county in which it appeared on the Democratic ballot, it passed with a 71% approval. Georgia is the first state in the nation where voters have said yes to the Personhood question. http://www.personhood.net/index.php?option=com_content&view=article&id=269&Itemid=649

18   They have signed a Georgia Right to Life Candidate Affirmation form which states: "[W]e believe, in the face of compelling biological evidence, that a continuum of human life and personhood begins at the moment of fertilization and ends at natural death, the ethical treatment of human embryos must include their "best interests. . . . [A]s a candidate for public office, I affirm my support for a Human Life Amendment to the Georgia Constitution and other actions that would support these principles. This would assure that regardless of race, age, degree of disability, manner of conception or circumstances surrounding a terminal illness, that the civil rights of the preborn at an embryonic or fetal level, the elderly and those with mental or physical infirmities are protected by law and are violated when we allow destructive embryonic stem cell research, therapeutic or

reproductive cloning, animal human hybrids, abortion (except to save the life of the mother), infanticide, euthanasia or assisted suicide."

19   *Defending Life 2010: Proven Strategies for a Prolife America*, p. 509.

20   Clarke D. Forsythe, *Politics for the Greatest Good: The Case for Prudence in the Public Square* (Downers Grove, Ill.: InterVarsity Press, 2009), pp. 25-27: "[A]n Aristolian evaluation of human nature may be one of the most effective ways to explain human nature." "Aristotle identifies four cardinal virtues: prudence, justice, courage and temperance." "Some Christians became skeptical of the importance of the cardinal virtues because of their classical or pagan roots. . . . They warily regarded it as too philosophical and not Scriptural enough." This is but a small sampling of the many references to Aristotle as the model of political wisdom through prudence. I studied at L'Abri with Dr. Francis Schaeffer in the summer of 1973. Dr. Schaeffer was fond of saying that the Bible is true truth but not exhaustive truth. It is completely true about everything to which it speaks, but it does not speak about everything there is to know. I am not opposed to extra-biblical truth as a guide, but I am opposed to it as an authority and as a defacto justification of moral cowardice and reductionist orthopraxy.

21   Dr. Martin Luther King Jr., "Letter from a Birmingham Jail," African Studies Center, University of Pennsylvania (16 April, 1963), http://www.africa.upenn.edu/Articles_Gen/Letter_Birmingham.html (accessed 2 December 2010).

22   Wikipedia, http://en.wikipedia.org/wiki/Natural_law (accessed 15 November 2010): "As classically used, natural law refers to the use of reason to analyze human nature and deduce binding rules of moral behavior."

23   Beginning here and throughout my use of the term "divine law" has the same basis as William Wilberforce's use in the following quote: "Policy, however, Sir, is not my principle, and I am not ashamed to say it. There is a principle above everything that is politic, and when I reflect on the command which says: 'Thou shalt do no murder,' believing its authority to be divine, how can I dare to set up any reasonings of my own against it."

24   Forsythe, 24-25: "The understanding of prudence (or practical wisdom) developed over time from Plato to Aristotle to Thomas Aquinas. Significant reflections on the meaning and importance of prudence start with Greek philosophy." Christianity should reject the premise that the practical godly wisdom of prudence originates with pagan Greek philosophy. Scripture tells

us that God's ways and man's ways are entirely opposite (Isaiah 55:8-9). Faith *and* reason originate from God: "The fear of the LORD is the beginning of wisdom." While some pagan philosophers, such as Cicero, acknowledged this, natural law does not.

25   Voltaire's *Dictionnaire Philosophique* (1764): "*Le mieux est l'ennemi du bien.*"

26   RenewAmerica.com, http://www.renewamerica.com/columns/brown/091210, (accessed 13 January 2011).

27   Georgia's HLA was not the first instance of activists trying to promote Personhood at a state level; at least two other times voter initiatives were attempted. On November 1, 2005 prolifer Dave (David) Rogers of Biloxi, Mississippi, introduced the Ultimate Human Life Amendment(UHLA), the first state Personhood amendment in American history. At around the same time Cal Zastrow cofounded Michigan Citizens for Life with the expressed goal of raising 315,000 signatures to place a Human Life amendment on the Michigan ballot.

28   Georgia General Assembly, http://www1.legis.ga.gov/legis/2007_08/search/hr536.html, (accessed 13 January 2011).

29   Courtroom Friezes: East and West Walls, http://www.supremecourt.gov/about/east&westwalls.pdf, (accessed January 29,2011).

30   "For when Gentiles, who do not have the law, by nature do what the law requires, they are a law to themselves, even though they do not have the law. They show that the work of the law is written on their hearts, while their conscience also bears witness, and their conflicting thoughts accuse or even excuse them that day when, a according to my gospel, God judges the secrets of men by Christ Jesus" (Romans 2:14-16).

31   U.S. Declaration of Independence (1776): "We hold these truths to be self-evident, that all men are created equal, that they are endowed by their Creator with certain unalienable rights, that among these are life, liberty and the pursuit of happiness."

32   Wikipedia, http://en.wikipedia.org/wiki/Natural_law (accessed 15 November 2010): "As classically used, natural law refers to the use of reason to analyze human nature and deduce binding rules of moral behavior."

33   America's Declaration of Independence, (1776), Three of the four references to God are theological in nature and can *not* be deduced from natural law 1. "that all men are created equal . . . endowed by their Creator with certain unalienable rights"; 2."to the Supreme Judge of the world for the rectitude

of our intentions"; 3. "to the protection of divine Providence"; 4. The other reference is acknowledging natural law, "the Laws of Nature and Nature's God". It is of additional interest that our U.S. Constitution was dated "the year of our Lord".

34 *The American Founding as the Best Regime: The Bonding of Civil and Religious Liberty* (1990), http://www.claremont.org/publications/pubid.682/pub_detail.asp, (accessed 14 January 2011).

35 Ibid.

36 *de Legibus*, Book 1.

37 Clarke Forsythe of AUL lobbied our legislature to defeat our Human Life Amendment. He stated that the exercise was imprudent. He justifies his action by over 30 references in his recent book, *Politics for the Greatest Good* to Thomas Aquinas' teaching on prudence.

38 Professor Charles Rice of Notre Dame, *50 Questions on the Natural Law,* (Ignatius Press, 1993), "Saint Thomas [Aquinas] places the human law within the context of the natural law and places them both within the overall design of God, the 'Chief Governor.' By contrast, the secular jurisprudence of the Enlightenment attempts to organize society as if God and his revelation did not exist. If it talks about natural law, that law is a secular version divorced from the divine law."

39 American Bible Society. (1992). The Holy Bible : The Good news Translation (2nd ed.) (Dt 24:16). New York: American Bible Society.

40 The Hebrew word for "man" (*adam*) is the generic term for humankind and, hence, the proper name Adam.

41 *Dred Scott v. Sanford*, 60 U.S. 393 (1856).

42 *Bailey & als. v. Poindexter's Ex'or*, 14 Grattan 432 (1858).

43 *The American Law Review.* 15 (January 1881): 21-37, 162.

44 Harry Blackmum, U.S. Supreme Court, *Roe v. Wade* (1973).

45 Andrew Pollack, "Engineering by Scientists on Embryo Stirs Criticism," *New York Times* (13 May 2008), http://www.nytimes.com/2008/05/13/science/13embryo.html (accessed 13 November 2010).

46 See Appendix 1, "Prolife Passages in Scripture."

47 W. E. Vine, M. F. Unger, and W. White, *Vine's Complete Expository Dictionary of Old and New Testament Words* (Nashville: Thomas Nelson, 1996), p. 307.

48 Wayne Grudem, *Systematic Theology* (Grand Rapids, Mich.: Zondervan Publishing House, 1994). Chapter 21:1-12.

49 Ibid.

50 *Didache*, A.D. 95.

51 George Grand, *Third Time Around: a history of the prolife movement from the first century to the present* (Brentwood, Tenn.: Wolgemuth & Hyatt Publishers, 1991), pp. 25-27.

52 Ibid.

53 Neocutis, "Technology," n.d., http://www.neocutis.com/categories.php?catid=11 (accessed 1 March 2010).

54 Dr. Amy Tuteur, n.d., http://open.salon.com/blog/amytuteurmd/2009/11/02/skin_cream_made_from_aborted_fetus (accessed 1 March 2010).

55 *Hagia Damhait*, 3.15.

56 Grant, p. 35.

57 Ibid.

58 *Code of Justinian*, 18.51-52.

59 Grant, p. 45.

60 Ibid.

61 John Boswell, *The Kindness of Strangers: The Abandonment of Children in Western Europe from Late Antiquity to the Renaissance* (New York: Pantheon Books, 1988).

62 Grant, pp. 55-56.

63 Ibid., p. 56.

64 WordIQ.com., http://www.wordiq.com/definition/Jean-Jacques_Rousseau (accessed 15 September 2010).

65 George Santayana, *Reason in Common Sense,* Volume One of The Life of Reason (New York: Dover Publications, 1980).

66 "About 40 Percent of American Women Have Had Abortions: The Math Behind the Stat," *Newsweek online,* http://www.newsweek.com/blogs/the-human-condition/2010/03/04/about-40-percent-of-american-women-have-had-abortions-the-math-behind-the-stat.html (accessed 16 September 2010).

67 "Generally speaking, the countries with the lowest rates are countries in Western Europe (e.g., Belgium has 111 abortions per 1000 live births; France 263:1000). Countries in Eastern Europe can have abortion rates that are ten times higher (e.g., Russia 1416:1000 and Romania 1156:1000)," http://www.euro.who.int/_data/assets/pdf_file/0004/69763/en59.pdf (accessed 16 September 2010).

68 John Calvin, leader of the Swiss Reformation, A.D. 1509-1564.

69 Ignatius Loyola, leader of the Catholic Counter Reformation, A.D. 1491–1556.

70   Grant, p. 72.

71   Anna Bowden, *Missionary Journals* (London: Sunday Schools Association for Overseas Missions, 1896): 1:11.

72   Grant, p. 72.

73   *Alexander Loce v. The State of New Jersey. On Petition for Writ of Certiorari to the Supreme Court of New Jersey*, Supreme Court of the United States, No. 92-1934 (October Term, 1993).

74   Mother Teresa of Calcutta, "Notable and Quotable," *Wall Street Journal* (February 25, 1994): A14.

75   Cornell University Law School, http://www.law.cornell.edu/supct/search/ display.html?terms=privacy%20AND%20penumbra&url=/supct/html/ historics/USSC_CR_0381_0479_ZO.html (accessed 22 September 2010).

76   Ibid.

77   http://www.ushistory.org/declaration/document (accessed 22 September 2010).

78   Mother Teresa of Calcutta.

79   Robert P. George and Christopher Tollefsen, in their book titled *Embryo: A Defense of Human Life* (New York: Doubleday, 2008), p.143, say "[T]he arguments of this book do not rely on any premise, claim, or authoritative teaching of any form of revealed religion." Noted prolife apologist Wesley Smith specifically made the point to the GRTL-sponsored May *2008: Personhood Symposium* that "none of his defense of Personhood was spiritual in nature." Seldom do you find a right to life ministry that is "faith-based." Georgia Right to Life elected unashamedly to embrace a "faith-based" basis of ministry in 2001.

80   Georgia Right to Life PAC has one of the highest and most rigid standards of endorsement in the nation for candidates seeking a right-to-life endorsement. Rape and incest exceptions are not permitted. The candidate must agree, 100%, with our stated prolife positions. The empirical data from Georgia Right to Life PAC, spanning a decade, has consistently shown that the most pragmatic course of action is to raise the standard to a biblical level and demand all politicians to meet that standard or risk defeat at the polls.

81   Clarke D. Forsythe, *Politics for the Greatest Good: The Case for Prudence in the Public Square* (Downers Grove, Ill.: InterVarsity Press, 2009). Aristotle is quoted more often than any other primary source.

82   It was offered in 46 counties on the Republican primary ballot of July 2010. In all 46 counties where the amendment was presented, it passed

overwhelmingly by an amazing 75 %! The one county where it appeared on the Democratic ballot it passed with 71% approval. Georgia is the first state in the nation where voters have said yes to the Personhood question.

83   http://www.Personhood.net/index.php?option=com_content&view=article &id=269&Itemid=649.

84   "Rock Art in Arkansas" (July 21, 2006), http://arkarcheology.uark.edu/ rockart/index.html?pageName=Glossary (accessed 1 March 2010).

85   Henry L. Chambers Jr., *Dred Scott: Tiered Citizenship and Tiered Personhood,* Introduction (April 12, 2007), http://www.cklawreview.com/wp-content/ uploads/vol82no1/Chambers.pdf (accessed 17 May 2010).

86   NRLC's Pain-Capable Unborn Child Protection Act is another example of a bill that focus' attention on the unborn child, as opposed to Americans United for Life emphasis on women's health.

87   *Human Dignity in the Biotech Century: a Christian vision for public policy,* edited by Charles W. Colson and Nigel M. de S. Cameron. (Downers Grove, Ill.: InterVarsity Press, 2004), p. 26.

88   Ronald Bailey, "The Pursuit of Happiness, Peter Singer interviewed by Ronald Bailey,"   http://reason.com/archives/2000/12/01/the-pursuit-of-happiness-peter , 2000, 1 (accessed 11 November 2010).

89   Ibid.

90   Ibid.

91   In a conversation with the author in May 2008 at Georgia Personhood Symposium.

92   Andrew Pollack, "Engineering by Scientists on Embryo Stirs Criticism," *New York Times* (13 May 2008), http://www.nytimes.com/2008/05/13/ science/13embryo.html (accessed 13 November 2010).

93   My prolife organization, Georgia Right to Life, has produced a website at Personhood.net in our attempt to engage the 21st century with a clear "Sanctity of Human Life" foundation. I would encourage you to familiarize yourself with its resources and message.

94   Ray Kurzweil, *The Singularity is Near* (Penguin Books, 2005), p. 11.

95   Michael J. Sleasman, "The Center for Bioethics & Human Dignity," n.d., http://cbhd.org/content/thinking-through-technology-part-i (accessed 11 March 2010).

96   *Nanoscale: Issues and Perspectives for the Nano Century*, edited by Nigel M. de S. Cameron and M. Ellen Mitchell (John Wiley & Sons, 2007), p. 9.

97   Ibid., p. 4.

98   Clarke D. Forsythe, *Politics for the Greatest Good: The Case for Prudence in the Public Square* (Downers Grove, Ill.: InterVarsity Press, 2009), p. 24.

99   David J. Vaughan, *Statesman and Saint, The Principled Politics of William Wilberforce* (Nashville: Cumberland House Publishing, 2002), pp. 257-258.

100 Findlaw.com., http://caselaw.lp.findlaw.com/scripts/getcase.pl?court=US&vol=000&invol=05-380#opinion1 (accessed 27 November 2010).

101 It is widely reported that over 90% of all children diagnosed with Down Syndrome are being aborted through a diagnostic test known as pre-implantation genetic diagnosis. An additional fact is that the test is known to produce as high as 10% false positives.

102 On January 22, 2003, ABCNEWS /*Washington Post* conducted a poll that showed that 69% of Americans oppose partial birth abortions. In 2010 Georgia's actual voting data shows that on average 75% of Georgia's Republican and 71% of the state's Democratic primary voters support Personhood.

103 Vaughan, p. 258.

104 Eric Metaxas, *Amazing Grace* (New York: HarperCollins Publishers, 2007), pp. 253-254.

105 PersonhoodUSA.com., http://Personhoodeducation.org/legal-resources (accessed 11 December 2010).

106 Forsythe, p. 254.

107 John Wilke, *Abortion: Questions and Answers* (Hayes Publishing Company, 1985), p. 3.

108 Ibid., 3-4.

109 Additional funding came from the Missouri Citizens for Life Educational Trust Fund and the Pallottine Center for Apostolic Causes.

110 *Restoring the Right to Life: The Human Life Amendment,* edited by James Bopp Jr. (Brigham Young University Press, 1984), p. viii.

111 James Bopp Jr., and Richard E. Coleson, *Prolife Strategy Issues* (August 7, 2007).

112 Ibid., p. 3.

113 See Appendix 2 for data from Georgia Right to Life from 2000-2010.

114 *Defending Life 2010: Proven Strategies for a Prolife America* (Washington, D.C.: Americans United for Life, 2010), p. 509.

115 Former Congressman Nathan Deal was able to overcome an 11-point deficit in the polls, only one week out, to win by 2,500 votes. 579,551 votes were

cast. What was amazing is that his opponent publicly attacked Georgia Right to Life's endorsement process for disqualifying her "prolife" claims, partly on the basis that she held "rape and incest" exceptions and thought Personhood was wrong for Georgia. Her defeat was also significant because she was endorsed by a very popular Sarah Palin. In the 2002 gubernatorial race FOX News conducted an exit poll declaring that 5.86% of *all* voters chose victor Sonny Perdue for the *sole* reason that he was prolife. If the same percentage were applied to this race (and we believe that this prolife metric in Georgia has increased since 2002), it would indicate that 34,000 votes were cast on the life issue alone . . . far in excess of Deal's 0.2% margin of victory. http://sos.georgia.gov/elections/election_results/2010_0810/0020001.html

116 It was offered in 46 counties on the Republican Primary Ballot of July 2010. In all 46 counties where the amendment was presented, it passed overwhelmingly, by an amazing 75%! In the one county where it appeared on the Democratic ballot it passed with 72% approval. Georgia is the first state in the nation where voters have said yes to the Personhood question. http://www.Personhood.net/index.php?option=com_content&view=article&id=269&Itemid=649

117 As reported in 2009 by Mary Boyert, director of Respect Life for the Archdiocese of Atlanta.

118 Theodore Roosevelt, "The Man in The Arena," Speech at the Sorbonne, Paris, France, April 23, 1910.

119 http://www.brainyquote.com/quotes/quotes/m/mothertere399948.html (accessed 22 September 2010).

120 http://www.brainyquote.com/quotes/quotes/m/mothertere114248.html (accessed 22 September 2010).

121 William Gothard, Institute in Basic Life Principles Seminar, Oak Brook, Illinois, explaining 2 Corinthians 10:11-13: "Let such a person understand that what we say by letter when absent, we do when present. Not that we dare to classify or compare ourselves with some of those who are commending themselves. But when they measure themselves by one another and compare themselves with one another, they are without understanding."

But we will not boast beyond limits, but will boast only with regard to the area of influence God assigned to us, to reach even to you."

122 Gualberto Garcia Jones, "Prudence and Moral Clarity in the Quest for Personhood," http://Personhoodeducation.files.wordpress.com/2009/06/prudence-education.pdf

123 Robert Muise, http://Personhood.net/legalconsiderations.html#introduction (accessed 27 November 2010).

124 James Bopp Jr., "Memorandum regarding Prolife Strategy Issues," James Bopp Jr. and Richard E. Coleson. Bopp, Coleson & Bostrom, August 21, 2007.

125 Attorneys Richard Thompson, Robert Muise, and Brian Rooney, Thomas More Law Center; David Gibbs III, attorney for Terri Schiavo, Christian Law Association; Attorney Barbara Weller, Gibbs Law Firm; Attorney Rita Dunaway, The Rutherford Institute; Dean of Law Mat Staver, Liberty Counsel; Attorney Jim Sedlak, American Life League; John Eidsmoe, Professor of Law, Oak Brook College of Law and Government Policy; and Attorney Walter Weber, American Center for Law and Justice.

126 Legislature of Nebraska. January 21, 2010, n.d., http://www.nebraska-legislature.gov/FloorDocs/101/PDF/Slip/LB1103.pdf, (accessed 31 January 2011).

127 Jill Stanek blog, http://www.jillstanek.com/2010/02/national-right-to-life-hopes-fetal-pain-bill-will-trigger-us-supreme-court-ruling/ (accessed 12 Decemeber 2010).

128 Randy Beck, "Where's the Syllogism?: Gonzales, Casey and the Viability Rule," ExpressO, 2007, available at http://works.bepress.com/randy_beck/1, 2 (accessed 4 December 2010).

129 Ibid., p. 22.

130 *Stenberg v. Carhart*, 530 U.S. 914, 962 (2000; J. Kennedy dissenting; citing *Washington v. Glucksberg*, 521 U.S. 702, 730-734 [1997]).

131 Beck, p. 26.

132 Legislature of Nebraska, http://www.jillstanek.com/2010/02/national-right-to-life-hopes-fetal-pain-bill-will-trigger-us-supreme-court-ruling/ (accessed 4 December 2010).

133 Gallup. http://www.gallup.com/poll/128036/new-normal-abortion-americans-prolife .aspx (accessed 4 December 2010).

134 Strategic Vision, http://www.strategicvision.biz/political/georgia_poll_110606.html. Question 11 (accessed 4 December 2010).

135 Declaration of Independence: "That to secure these rights, Governments are instituted among Men, deriving their just powers from the consent of the governed."

136 President Abraham Lincoln, Gettysburg Address, November 19,1863.

137 Republican U.S. Senatorial candidate Ken Buck, 2010.

138 http://www.grtl.org/docs/prolifeprinciples.pdf

139 http://www.grtl.org/2010Candidates.asp

140 The most recent occasion was the former speaker of our House Glenn Richardson, who single-handedly shut down our attempt to pass the human life amendment in 2008. He fell into a depression after a very public moral lapse in 2009 and attempted to take his own life. Within a month he had resigned the most powerful political post in Georgia. This is not an isolated example.

141 "New Abortion Wars: An age-old fight is heating up in the state," *U.S. News and World Report* (January 8, 2008), http://politics.usnews.com/news/politics/articles/2008/01/03/new-abortion-wars.html?PageNr=2 (accessed 12 December 2010).

142 Bret Schulte, "New Abortion Wars," *U.S. News & World Report* (January 14, 2008), p. 21.

143 Ibid., p. 23, Rep. Martin Scott was the sponsor of the Human Life Amendment in Georgia in 2007.

144 Campaign 2008 C-Span, August 27, 2008, as viewed on Youtube.Com, *Republican Platform "Research" Amendment*, http://www.youtube.com/watch?v=7juKiUNbsz8 (accessed 18 December 2010). At timestamp 3:00 minutes, ". . . there is therapeutic research that can be done on human embryos, and there is nothing inethical, immoral, improper . . . or that disregards the sanctity of human life, if we are involved in therapeutic research. The placing the 'or' here however, means that all quote 'experimentation' on human embryos for research purposes should be banned including therapeutic research, and that is wrong, so I oppose the amendment."

145 Stephen Spruiell , "Going Out with a Bang," National Review Online, August 27, 2008, http://www.nationalreview.com/corner/168039/going-out-bang/stephen-spruiell (accessed 18 December 2010).

146 SB 169, The Ethical Treatment of Human Embryos, http://www.legis.state.ga.us/legis/2009_10/sum/sb169.html (accessed 18 December 2010).

147 Deuteronomy 19:10, Deuteronomy 19:13, Deuteronomy 21:8, Deuteronomy 21:9, Deuteronomy 27:25, 1 Samuel 19:5, 1 Kings 2:5, 1 Kings 2:31, 2 Kings 21:16, 2 Kings 24:4, Psalm 94:21, Psalm 106:38, Proverbs 6:17, Isaiah 9:5, Isaiah 59:7, Jeremiah 7:6, Jeremiah 19:4, Jeremiah 22:3, Jeremiah 22:17, Jeremiah 26:15, Lamentations 4:13, Joel 3:19, Jonah 1:14, Matthew 23:35, Matthew 27:4.

148 *Bloodguilt*, The Jewish Virtual Library, American-Israeli Cooperative Enterprise, http://www.jewishvirtuallibrary.org/jsource/judaica/ejud_0002_0003_0_03145.html, (accessed 17 January 2011).

149 Robert A. Rutland, ed., *The Papers of George Mason* (Chapel Hill: The University of North Carolina Press, 1970), pp. 965-966. This statement reiterated and expanded Mason's views at the Constitutional Convention on August 22.

150 Currently a fringe proposition, run by fringe proponents, the future must certainly contain advances in the development of a practical hydrogen fuel cell that would solve our energy needs. http://waterpoweredcar.com/ (accessed 1 January 2011).

151 PSFK, *XWave App: Control An iPhone With Your Mind, Mind Interface for the iPhone,* http://www.psfk.com/2011/01/xwave-app-control-an-iphone-with-your-mind.html (accessed 30 January 2011).

152 Defense Advanced Research Projects Agency (DARPA), http://www.darpa. mil/news/2010/DeepLearningReleaseFinal.pdf (accessed 19 December 2010).

153 Ibid.

154 http://www.singularity.com/ (accessed 19 December 2010).

155 http://en.wikipedia.org/wiki/Turing_test (accessed 19 December 2010).

156 MIT's Institute for Soldier Nanotechnologies (ISN), http://web.mit.edu/ isn/partners/industry/currentpartners.html (accessed 24 December 2010).

157 World Transhumanist Association, http://www.transhumanism.org/index. php/WTA/more/1279/ (accessed 24 December 2010).

158 H+ Magazine, http://humanityplus.org/, accessed 24 December 2010).

159 While it is technically true that the name of Cain's wife is not mentioned specifically, the term "wife" in Hebrew is "ishshah." I took literary license based on the Hebrew word for man being "adam," hence the proper name of the first man, Adam. For a word study of "ishshah" see http://www.searchgodsword. org/isb/view.cgi?number=0802 (accessed 24 December 2010).

160 This is not an allusion to a homosexual relationship. The 22nd century is not only post-human, it is also post-gender.

161 Peter Aldhous, "Are male eggs and female sperm on the horizon?" *New Scientist* (February 2, 2008), http://www.geneticsandsociety.org/article. php?id=3904 (accessed 24 December 2010).

162 Sacha Zimmerman, "ECTOGENESIS: Development of Artificial Wombs Technology's threat to abortion rights," *San Francisco Chronicle* (August 24, 2003), http://www.sfgate.com/cgi-bin/article.cgi?f=/c/a/2003/08/24/ IN273768.DTL (accessed 24 December 2010): "[R]esearchers estimate that ectogenesis could be a reality within five years."

163 Cindy Kuzma, "Of Manimals and Humanzees," *Science & Spirit* (January 17, 2007), http://www.freerepublic.com/focus/f-news/1769379/posts (accessed 24 December 2010).

164 Peter W. Singer, "How to Be All That You Can Be: A Look at the Pentagon's Five Step Plan For Making Iron Man Real," The Brookings Institution, http://www.brookings.edu/articles/2008/0502_iron_man_singer.aspx (accessed 24 December 2010).

165 GRASP (Great Ape Standing & Personhood), http://www.personhood.org/ (accessed 24 December 2010).

166 "First Self-Replicating Synthetic Bacterial Cell," Press Release, J. Craig Venter Institute (May 21, 2001), http://www.jcvi.org/cms/press/press-releases/full-text/article/first-self-replicating-bacterial-cell-constructed-by-j-craig-venter-institute-researcher/ (accessed 1 January 2011).

167 Jerome C. Glenn, "2010 State of the Future, Millennium Project," http://www.millennium-project.org/ (accessed 1 January 2011): "**The Millennium Project** was founded in 1996 after a three-year feasibility study with the United Nations University, Smithsonian Institution, Futures Group International, and the American Council for the UNU. It is now an independent non-profit global participatory futures research think tank of futurists, scholars, business planners, and policy makers who work for international organizations, governments, corporations, NGOs, and universities. The Millennium Project manages a coherent and cumulative process that collects and assesses judgments from over 2,500 people since the beginning of the project selected by its 38 Nodes around the world. The work is distilled in its annual 'State of the Future,' 'Futures Research Methodology' series, and special studies."

168 Nigel Cameron, "Germline Intervention," Institute on Biotechnology and the Human Future, http://www.thehumanfuture.org/topics/germline_intervention/ (accessed 1 January 2011).

169 As of 2010 the University of Copenhagen is working on creating a synthetic hybrid of protein and DNA. Their goal is to update humanity's existing two-strand DNA helix to a three-strand, triple helix Peptide Nucleic Acid (PNA).

170 This is reputed to have actually happened, although it is reported to have only pierced a Level One or a Level Two lab at the CDC off Clifton Road.

171 You can actually order a T-shirt spoofing the event at "The Monkeys are Loose," http://www.cafepress.com/+reemco_cdc_ebola_outbreak_organic_cotton_tshirt,11847127.

172 University of Southern California, Initiative & Referendum Institute, http://
www.iandrinstitute.org/New%20IRI%20Website%20Info/Drop%20
Down%20Boxes/Requirements/Almanac%20-%20Signature%20and%20
SS%20and%20GD%20Requirements.pdf (accessed 5 January 2011).

173 Preface to *Issues in Law and Medicine* (Spring 2010), editor-in-chief James
Bopp Jr.

Acknowledgments

There are many friends who have contributed generously of their time, talents and resources to assure that this message gets a proper hearing.

I want to thank

Judy Becker, by being a godly example you have paved the way and encouraged another generation of authors.

The past president of Georgia Right to Life, Caryl Swift, the board of directors and my dedicated staff for supporting my work on this book.

Jan and Greg Winchester, who graciously gifted me a week of undisturbed solitude in an idyllic getaway home. That proved to be the catalyst needed to jump-start the whole project.

The elders of Grace Fellowship for their oversight, counsel and support, without which, I would not dare enter into the fray.

Daniel Woodard, a visionary on behalf of the unborn.

Gualberto Garcia, for providing much of the material on ballot initiatives, their history and effectiveness.

Cal Zastrow, for launching this project with an offhanded challenge and a "Praise the Lord".

Keith Mason, whose partnership and encouragement is a blessing.

Professor Charles Rice and Rob Muise, whose academic and legal counsel provided much needed help in areas of Catholic thought and doctrine.

Karen LaBarr and Gen Wilson for spending hours providing needful edits and corrections. All remaining errors are solely mine.

My grown family of five children, their spouses and my twenty-six grandchildren whose most common question is "Grandpa is your book finished yet, we need you to take us to IHOP?"

Index

A

abandonment/killing of deformed/ mentally disabled/unwanted children—52, 53, 56

Abolition of Man, The (see also "C. S. Lewis")—63

abolition of slavery—83, 86

Abolition Society—83

abortion—16, 22, 50, 51, 52, 56, 57, 59, 63, 71, 74, 77, 80, 84, 107, 109, 114, 121, 128, 141

abortion guide—51

abortion mill—59

abortion on demand—15

Abortion, Questions and Answers (see also "Wilke, Dr. Jack")—33, 89

abortion rate, per capita—25

abortion rights, basis for—45, 71

Adamnan of Ions—54

Aegidius, Giles—55

African-American community—25

Alzheimers—21, 23, 74, 75

Amazing Grace (see also "Metaxis, Eric")—85

"amelioration" argument—85

American Center for Law and Justice—89

American Civil Liberties Union (ACLU)—15

American Civil War—127

American Law Review, The (see also "Canfield, George F.")—44

American Life League—35

Americans for Tax Reform—106

Americans United for Life—87

amicus curiae (friend of the court)—59

anti-abortion focus of prolife movement in twentieth century—74, 75

Antwerp—53

Aquinas, Thomas (see also *Treatise on Law*)—38, 39

Aristotle—28, 34, 40, 55, 61, 62, 82

artificial intelligence—132

Arya Samaj—58

atonement of Jesus Christ—125, 126

B

Balch, Burke—34

Balch, Mary—97

ballot initiatives—35, 104, 105, 106, 107, 108, 109, 110, 115

ban on abortion (different possible conditions/levels)—114

ban on cloning 75, 122

ban on embryonic stem cell research—122

ban on in-vitro vertilization—123

Basil of Caesarea—51, 52

Bathild of Chelles, Princess—54

Beck, Randy—98, 99

"best as enemy of good"—34, 40, 67

biblical worldview—69, 80, 141

Bill of Rights—61

bioethical concerns—78

biomedical research—62, 63

bio-policy—79

Biotech age/century—77, 141

biotech industry / biotechnology—76, 77, 129

black colleges/universities—25

Blackmun, Harry—45, 91

Blacks / Black race—44, 70, 77, 78

Blackstone, William (see also *Lex Rex*) —38

blindness—103

"blob of tissue"—57, 71

bloodguilt in Bible—126

Boehlert, Sherwood—79

Bojaxhiu, Agnes Gonxha (Mother Teresa)—59

Bonaventure—55

Boniface of Crediton—54

Bopp, James, Jr.—70, 89, 90, 95, 96, 97, 122, 123, 124

Borden, Sir Robert—45

"born persons"—77

Boswell, John—56

Bound for Life—128

Bowden, Anna—58, 59

British North America Act—45

Brown, Judie—35

Bryant, David—128

Buddhism—42

Burton, Kristi—35, 45

Bush, George Sr.—17

C

Caelrhyn, Dympna—52

Calcutta—59

Calvin, John—57

Cameron, Nigel—79

Campaign Tracker—112

Canadian Charter of Rights—33, 89

Canadian Supreme Court—45

Canfield, George F.—44

Casey v. Planned Parenthood—97

Catholic encyclicals—62

cell bank—52

Center for Bio-ethical Reform—44

Center for Biotechs & Human Dignity—78

chemical abortion (see also "self-administered abortion")—56, 57, 71

Chesterton, G. K.—120

child sacrifice—56, 63, 118

chimera (see also "human-animal hybrid," "'glow-in-the-dark' human embryo")—22, 76, 78

"choice"—16, 119

Christian culture of life (see also "culture of life")—50

Christian homes for pagan temple prostitutes—51

Christian homes for unwed mothers—51

Christian orphanages—51

Church, the—14, 28, 50, 53, 55, 56, 57, 61, 62, 67, 80, 95, 120

Church Age—50, 52

Church history—50, 53, 57, 73, 91, 95

Church in the Middle Ages—52, 53

Cicero—28, 39, 55, 67

civil rights movement—31

Claremont Graduate School—38

Clinton, Bill—17

cloning—22, 71, 80, 102

cloning for "therapeutic" purposes— 75, 124

Colorado—87, 108, 109, 120, 121

Colorado Catholic Conference—108

Colorado Right to Life—120

"coming of age"—41
Concerts of Prayer—128
conscience—71
Constitutional Convention—44
constitutional republic—103
contraceptives—61
Cornell University—22, 45, 76
Counter Reformation—57
Coverdell, Paul—119
crisis pregnancy—50
Cryer, Catherine (CNN program)—15
"crystal ball" argument—98
cultic abortifacient procedures
    (*kananda*)—58
culture of death—52, 77, 100
culture of life (see also "Christian
    culture of life")—24, 50
Cunningham, Gregg—16
Cuthbert of Lindisfarne—55
cyborgs (human-machine cybrids)—78

D

"Dark Ages" (see also "Middle
    Ages")—53
David (biblical)—14, 55, 119
deafness—103
Declaration of Independence—38, 69
"defective infant"—74
Delaware—105
dependency—24, 53, 80
designer babies—78
"devil's child"—52
deyana—58
Didache, The—43, 50, 51
Dignitatas Personae—62
disability, disabled—23, 50, 52, 53,
    62, 67, 74, 80, 84, 102, 103, 128
divine law—32, 34, 36, 37, 38, 39,
    40, 46, 82, 124, 126, 127
DNA—76

"Do evil that good may come"—84
Doe v. Bolten—15
Down Syndrome—84
Dred Scott v. Sanford—44, 70, 77
Druids—54
"due process" clause of Constitution—91
Dunstan of Canterbury—55

E

Eadburh, King—53
Edburga of Winchester—55
Edward the Confessor—55
elderly infirm—50, 56, 62, 67, 74, 84,
    128
Elizabeth of Portugal—55
emancipation of slaves—83, 86, 127
Embryo: A Defense of Human Life . . .—87
"embryo adoption" bill—93
embryonic stem cell research—102,
    113, 114, 122
embryos (harvested for human
    research)—56
encephalitis—103
end of life issues—113
endorsement criteria—18
Enlightenment, The—55
epilepsy—103
ethics of human nature—77
ethics of life and death—77
eugenics—71, 76, 78, 79, 84
euthanasia—22, 71
Evangelium Vitae—62
"exceptions"—26

F

Family Research Council—89, 90
Farmer Refuted, The (see also
    "Hamilton, Alexander")—37
fatherless society—60
fear—91, 92, 93, 94

federal funding for abortion—26

female infanticide (*deyana*)—58

"fencing in" abortion/evil—71, 83, 84, 100

fertility clinics—76

fetal biopsies—52

fetal tissue for medicinal/cosmetic purposes—52

50 Questions on Natural Law (see also "Rice, Charles")—39

"first do no harm"—96

Florida—99

Focus on the Family—90

Forsythe, Clarke—81, 82, 87, 88

40 Days of Life—128

Fox, Michael J.—75

Fox News—121

France and abortion—56

free speech censorship—16

G

Garn Amendment—90

gender—23

gene therapy (definition of)—76

genetic alteration of eggs or sperm—78

genocide in Nazi Germany—45

genome, human (alteration)—78

George, Robert—87

Georgia Conference of Catholic Bishops—39

Georgia Right to Life (GRTL)—17, 24, 28, 35, 39, 46, 66, 67, 90, 92, 94, 95, 97, 118, 121

Georgia State Constitution—68

Georgia State House—24, 115

Georgia State Senate—19, 124

Georgia's 9th U.S. House District—17, 18

Georgia's prolife history/status/success—20, 24, 27, 28, 40, 68, 84, 88, 92, 93, 95, 99, 100, 115, 118

"germ-line intervention"—78

Gheel—52, 53

Gibbs, David—89

"glow-in-the-dark" human embryo—22, 45, 76

godly wisdom—61, 66, 68, 91

God's institution of government—101, 118

Goliath—119

Gonzales v. Carhart—97, 98

Good King Wenceslas—54

Good Morning, America—15

governmental/legal definition of person; see also "person" (definition)—33, 39, 44, 45, 71, 76, 79, 80, 83, 96, 98, 108, 141

GPS—32

Grant, Dr. George (see also *Third Time Around*)—50

grassroots prolife voter/movement—75, 80

Graves, Tom—18

Gray, Nellie—34, 35

Greek philosophers/classical wisdom—55, 66

Gregory the Great—55

Griswold v. Connecticut—61

Grudem, Wayne—49

Gumbel, Bryant—15

H

H.R. 536—35

Haire, Father Robert W.—105

Hamilton, Alexander (see also *Farmer Refuted, The*)—37

Harvard Medical School—52

harvesting of human collagen for cosmetics—51

hedonism—136

Hindu extremism—58

Hinduism—43, 58
Hitler, Adolph—102
Holy Spirit—28, 47, 73
Homo perfectus—79
Homo sapiens—79
House Judiciary Committee—39
human-animal hybrid (see "chimera," "'glow-in-the-dark' human embryo")—22, 76, 78
human dignity—48, 49, 50, 62, 63, 70, 73, 75, 77, 80
human gene pool—78
human life amendment, federal (see also "Personhood amendment, federal")—32, 82, 90
Human Life Amendment, of Georgia—39, 95
human life amendment, state level—90
"human pesticide"—57
human rights—71, 121, 122
Humanae Vitae—62
Hyde Amendment—26, 27

I

Ignatius Loyola—57
illegitimacy—53, 56
image of God (see also "*Imago Dei*")—24, 37, 41, 42, 43, 49, 50, 63, 73, 77, 78, 80, 134
"image of Man"—63, 78
Imago Dei (see also "image of God")—42, 48, 49, 50, 61, 62, 64, 67, 69, 71, 73, 79
incarnation of Jesus Christ—49, 55
incest—80
incest exception (see also "rape exception")—24, 26, 27, 34, 71, 109, 113, 122
incrementalism / incremental gains/ legislation—56, 71, 82, 83, 84, 85, 113
India—58
Industrial Age—77
infanticide—50, 51, 52, 53, 74
infertility—76, 114
injunctive relief—16
Institute on Biotechnology & the Human Future—79
"Instructions" (Roman Catholic encyclicals)—62
in-vitro fertilization (IVF)—71, 76, 80, 113, 123
Isaiah (prophet)—47

J

Jaffa, Harry V.—38
Jefferson, Thomas—126, 127
Jeremiah (prophet)—47, 125
Jesus Christ (in humanist thought)—55
Jews (considered "subjects," not "citizens," by Nazi Germany)—45
Joash—126
John the Baptist—47, 73, 74
John of Amathus, Pastor—54
Jones, Gualberto Garcia—95, 110
Judeo-Christian concept of divine law—37
Judeo-Christian concept of law—42
Judeo-Christian construct of personhood—41, 76
justice/judgment of God—124, 125, 126, 128
Justinian of Byzantium—43, 53

K

kananda—58
Kennedy, Anthony—16, 84, 97, 98, 99
"killing fields"—80
King, Dr. Martin Luther, Jr.—31
kingdom of God—14

"kingmaker" paradigm—19, 94
Kolkata (Calcutta)—59
Koop, Dr. C. Everett—63
Kurtzwiel, Ray—77

L
L'Abri Fellowship—29
legislative propositions (see propositions)
"lesser authority"—61
Lewis, C. S. (see also *Abolition of Man, The*)—63
Lex Rex (see also "Blackstone, William")—38
Liberty Counsel—89
"Life Principles"—34
Limbaugh, Rush—15
Lincoln, Abraham—127
Loce, Alexander—59
Louis of France—55

M
Madedoc of Ferns—54
Manasseh—126
Mandatory Human Life Amendment (see also "human life amendment," "Personhood amendment")—34
Manhood—41
manner of conception (see also "illegitimacy")–24, 26, 39, 53, 71, 80, 122
March for Life—35
Margaret of Scotland—54, 55
Marty, Martin—105
martyrs—67
Mason, George—126
Mason, Keith—35, 109
"medical termination"—51
Medieval period (see also "Middle Ages")—52, 54
"mercy death"—102

Metaxis, Eric (see also *Amazing Grace*)—85
Michigan—19, 99
Michigan Right to Life—19
Middle Ages—28, 43, 52, 53, 55, 56, 61
Miller, Zell—118
Mills, James—119
Missouri—75
Missouri State Constitution—75
Montana—87
moral courage—95
moral cowardice—67, 87, 92
"moral perfectionism"—82
Morristown, NJ—59
Moses—55
Mother Teresa—29, 59, 60, 61, 94
Muise, Robert—38, 95, 96
Murphy, Emily—45
muscular spasticity—103

N
"nano-policy roundtable"—79
national atonement for sin—125
National Institutes of Health—45, 76
National Public Radio—15
National Review Online—122
National Right to Life Committee (NRLC)—19, 32, 33, 34, 70, 89, 91, 93, 96, 97, 99, 123
National Right to Life Committee Amendment—90
National Right to Life Educational Trust Fund—90
National Right to Life local affiliates—110
natural law—32, 34, 36, 37, 38, 39, 40, 46, 124
Nazi Germany—45, 77, 102
Nebraska fetal pain law (see also "Nebraska Pain-Capable Unborn

Child Protection Act")—97
Nebraska Pain-Capable Unborn Child
    Protection Act (see also "Nebraska
    fetal pain law")—97, 99
Neocutis—51
neo-pagan humanism—62, 63
neo-paganism—56, 102
neurological impairment—103
New Jersey—99
New Jersey v. Alexander Loce, et al.—59
New York Times—22
Nineteenth century—57
"no-exception" prolife stance—17, 19,
    24, 34, 68, 88, 109
noninterference policy in Britain—58
Norquist, Grover—106
North Carolina—122
Notre Dame—39
Notre Dame Law School—86
Nuclear Age—77
Nuremberg Laws on Citizenship and
    Race—45

O

Obama, Barak—100, 103
115 Forum—96
orphanage—56
orthodoxy v. orthopraxy—82

P

pagan culture of death—50
"pagan piety—87
paganism—28, 41, 44, 52, 55, 61, 62
Palin, Sarah—92
paralysis—103
parental consent for abortion—71
Parkinson's disease—75
Parliament—86
partial birth abortion—84, 85
Partial Birth Abortion Ban Act—84, 91

Paul, apostle—17, 28, 37, 41, 50, 55,
    66, 69, 82, 101, 103, 118, 124, 125
Penn, William—40
Pennsylvania—99
"person" (definition); see also
    "governmental definition"—21, 22,
    33, 37, 43, 44, 45, 74, 76, 77, 79,
    80, 83
persona—42, 43
Personhood—7, 20, 22, 23, 24, 25, 26,
    27, 28, 32, 33, 34, 36, 37, 39, 42,
    43, 44, 45, 46, 47, 57, 58, 59, 62,
    64, 65, 66, 67, 68, 69, 70, 71, 72,
    73, 74, 76, 77, 79, 80, 82, 83, 84,
    85, 86, 87, 89, 91, 92, 93, 96, 97,
    98, 100, 110, 111, 112, 113, 114,
    115, 120, 122, 124, 141
Personhood amendment,
    Colorado—108, 120, 121
Personhood amendment, federal (see
    also "human life amendment,
    federal")—82, 83, 89, 113, 114, 133
Personhood amendment,
    Georgia—17, 24, 68, 87, 92
Personhood amendment, non-binding
    straw poll in Georgia—27, 68, 92
Personhood amendment,
    Michigan—86
Personhood amendment, state—82, 113
Personhood Colorado—95
Personhood from biblical perspective—
    27, 28, 32, 35, 36, 37, 43, 44,
    46, 47, 48, 63, 69, 74, 76, 80,
    82, 95, 121
personhood in antiquity—41
Personhood in twentieth century—59
Personhood in twenty-first century—
    73, 75, 76, 93, 95, 121, 141
personhood of blacks—70, 77
personhood of dependent / mentally

impaired—80
personhood of disabled—80, 84, 103, 128
personhood of disabled infants—102
personhood of elderly infirm—84, 128
personhood of infants through 18 months of age—74, 80
personhood of Indians—44
personhood of slaves—83
personhood of test-tube embryos—76
personhood of unborn/preborn—27, 45, 69, 80, 84, 109, 128
personhood of women—44, 45
Personhood recognized vs. defined—43
Personhood, when designation attaches under law—59, 77, 95
PersonhoodUSA—35, 109, 112
Pitt Hames, Margie—15
"planned barrenness"—50
Planned Parenthood—39
Plato—28, 55
Political Action Committee (PAC)—111, 112
Political Action Committee of Georgia Right to Life—18
political compromise—19
politics and the Christian—104
polls—99, 100, 121
post-Christian—131
"post-human"—100, 129, 134
postmodern world—82
"post-person"—23
pragmatism—62
preborn—62, 67, 70, 71, 74
Pregnancy Resource Centers—25, 51
pre-implantation genetic diagnosis (PGD)—76
"pre-person"—23
Princeton University—21, 74
principled prudential pragmatism—83

Processed Skin Cell Proteins (PSP)—52
"procreative right"—75
Prohibition—25
"prolife" candidates/legislators (definition)—24, 26, 27, 34, 35, 113
proposition—105, 109
prudence—83, 84, 86, 87
prudence, biblical—81, 82, 91
Prunyard Shopping Ctr. v. Robins—95, 96
"psychological harm" to children—15
Pythagoras—55

Q

Queen Victoria—58
"quid pro quo"—19

R

race—23
rape—80
"rape and incest" position—18, 19, 93
rape exception (see also incest exception)—24, 26, 27, 34, 71, 109, 113, 122
reason—28, 29, 34, 37, 38, 46, 56
Reeve, Christopher—75, 102
referendums—104, 105, 106, 107, 109, 110
Reformation—57
relativism—62
Renaissance—28, 44, 55
"representation" (God-given human attribute)—48, 49
retardation—103
Rice, Charles (see also *50 Questions on Natural Law*)—39, 86
"right of abortion"—60
right to life—34, 60, 62, 63, 69, 74, 76, 77, 82
right to life as God-given—69, 70, 77

Right to Life movement—74, 75
"right to parent"—76
"right to privacy"—16, 61, 71, 91, 119
ritual sacrifice of widows (*sarti*)—58
Robert Powell Center for Medical Ethics—34
Roberts, Chief Justice—97, 98
Roe v. Wade—25, 26, 31, 33, 45, 60, 61, 70, 84, 91, 96, 97, 98, 99, 107, 108, 113
Roman Catholic Church—35, 62
Roman construct of personhood—42
Roman philosophers—55
Roman republic—103
Rome—51
Roosevelt, Theodore—93
Rousseau, Jean-Jacques—56

S

sacrament of marriage—48
sagae, the—51
"Saint of Calcutta" (Mother Teresa)—59
sanctity of life—25, 26, 27, 37, 47, 48, 49, 50, 53, 56, 57, 60, 63, 71, 73, 80, 114, 119, 141
sanctity of life ethic—50, 54, 59, 62, 68, 75, 91, 107
Santayana, George—56
sarti—58
Sava of Trnova—55
Schaeffer, Dr. Francis—29, 63, 66
SCNT (somatic cell nuclear transfer; see also cloning)—75, 80
Scott, Martin—17, 35, 121
secular humanism/worldview—55, 61, 74
selective reduction—76, 114
"self-administered" abortion (see also "chemical abortion")—57
Senate Health, Education, Labor and Pensions Committee—102
Seneca—28, 55
senility—103
"shadow government of Georgia"—28
Shaivo, Terri—89
Sherman, Brad—79
Sickle Cell Anemia—78
Singer, Peter (see also *Unsanctifying Human Life*)—21, 74
slave (as "non-person")—44, 83
Slave Registry Bill—86
slave trade—83, 85, 86
Slave Trade Act—84
slavery—84, 85
Sleasman, Michael—78
Slovensky, Clement—55
Smith, Wesley—74
Solomon—55
soul—42
South Dakota—87, 105
Spritzer, Marty—79
Spruiell, Stephen—122
"standard bearers" paradigm—19, 94
stem cell research—22
Stenberg case—98
Strategic Vision—99
strongholds (worldly)—14
Stupak, Congressman—26
Summa, Mary—122
surgical abortion—56, 71
Swift, Caryl—18
syncretism—61

T

T4 Aktion program—102
Tada, Joni Eareckson—23
Tay-Sachs—78
Tennessee—19
Teutonic tribes—54
"the sky is falling" argument—90, 96, 97, 98

Third Time Around (see also "Grant, Dr. George")—50

Thomas More Law Center—38, 89, 95

Time magazine—121

"timing argument"—91, 96

Today Show, The—15

Tollefson, Christopher—87

transgenic—76

trans-human enhancement—78

trans-human philosophers—79

transhumanism—79, 133

Treatise on Law (see also "Aquinas, Thomas")—38

Trinity—48

Truth (God's)—14, 66, 67, 78, 91, 95, 127

Tuteur, Dr. Amy—52

U

U.S. Congress—16

U.S. Congress of Catholic Bishops—35

U.S. Constitution—44, 61, 71, 83, 89, 96

U. S. House of Representatives—16, 20

U.S. House Science Committee—79

U.S. News and World Report—121

U.S. Supreme Court—15, 36, 44, 59, 69, 70, 77, 84, 90, 91, 96, 97, 98, 99

ultrasound—119

"unalienable" right to life—23, 24, 61, 69, 77

Unborn Victims of Violence Act—108

underground railroad—105

University of Georgia—98, 99

Unsanctifying Human Life (see also "Singer, Peter")—74

"useless eaters" —102

"using prior restraint"—16

utilitarianism—102, 103

V

Vatican Congregation for the Doctrine of the Faith (CDF)—62

Victorian era—59

victory of divine law over Roman law–43

Voltaire—34, 67

W

Washington (state)—99

Weinman, Adoph A.—36

Western law's concept of Personhood—44

Whatever Happened to the Human Race?—63

"white list"—112

Wilberforce, William—83, 85, 86

Willke, Dr. Jack (see also *Abortion, Questions & Answers*)—32, 89

women declared "non-persons" in Canada—44, 45

women's suffrage—105

worldly/secular/pagan wisdom—28, 39, 55, 56, 61, 62

Y

Yale University—56

Z

Zastrow, Cal—35, 109

Zechariah—125

"History will one day look upon the movement to affirm the personhood of unborn children in the same way we now look upon the abolition of slavery and the end of the Holocaust. Dan Becker has been a reliable and principled voice for the unborn. His book advancing personhood for the most vulnerable among us is like a sound of the trumpet that will reverberate throughout time. The Holocaust of the unborn is the darkest chapter in American history and Dan Becker's book is a call to turn the page and restore a culture of life. It is a must read."

Mathew D. Staver
Dean and Professor of Law
Liberty University School of Law

"'Personhood' is at the very heart of the 21st Century Civil Rights Movement. My Uncle Martin once said that to deny a person is " to say that he has no right to existence." Whether it is Dred Scott, Sojourner Truth, 1968 Sanitation Workers, or a baby viewed in a 3D Ultrasound, from conception until natural birth, a person is a human being, entitled to life, liberty and the pursuit of happiness. This right to personhood is a civil right. So, this book is an essential tool for these times."

Dr. Alveda C. King
(Niece of Dr. Martin Luther King, Jr.)
King for America
Priests for Life

For comprehensive and up-to-date coverage of the Personhood issue be sure and checkout www.personhood.net or for a more active role www.personhoodusa.com.

CPSIA information can be obtained at www.ICGtesting.com
Printed in the USA
LVOW081943260911

247984LV00001B/3/P